Canada's Colonies

A History of the Yukon
and Northwest Territories

James Lorimer & Company, Publishers
Toronto 1985

Cover design: Brant Cowie/Artplus
Cover photo: SSC Photocentre/K.-H. Raach
Maps: Brandon University Geography Department

Canadian Cataloguing in Publication Data

Coates, Kenneth, 1956-
   Canada's colonies: a history of the Yukon and Northwest Territories

(Canadian Issues Series)
ISBN 0-88862-932-X (bound). — ISBN 0-88862-931-1 (pbk.)

1. Yukon Territory — History. 2. Northwest Territories — History. I. Title. II. Series: Canadian issues series (Toronto, Ont.)

FC3956.C62 1985   971.9 C85-099401-2

F1090.5.C62 1985

James Lorimer & Company, Publishers
Egerton Ryerson Memorial Building
35 Britain Street
Toronto, Ontario M5A 1R7

Printed and bound in Canada

5 4 3 2 1   85 86 87 88 89

Contents

Acknowledgements

This book, like any other, has benefitted greatly from the advice and assistance of others. The enthusiasm and guidance of Ted Mumford of James Lorimer & Company has been most appreciated. Dr. R. Stuart and James Darlington provided useful comments on early drafts of the manuscript. Bruce Stadfeld offered help with research far beyond the call of duty. Special thanks are reserved for my colleague at Brandon University, Dr. W.R. Morrison, who read with care all the drafts of this work. While the help provided has no doubt strengthened this book, they are in no way responsible for errors which may remain in the text. Dr. Peter Hordern, Dean of Arts at Brandon University, was again generous in his support and encouragement. I owe thanks to the university's research committee for financial aid. My family, Cathy, Bradley, Mark and Laura, tolerated my lengthy absences with remarkable understanding. I would like to dedicate this book to my mother and father, Margaret and Richard Coates, who took me north and taught me to love the land and the people.

Ken Coates
Lake Clementi, Manitoba
August 1985

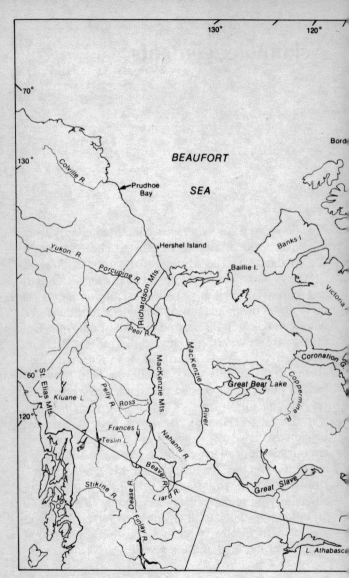

The North: Physical Features

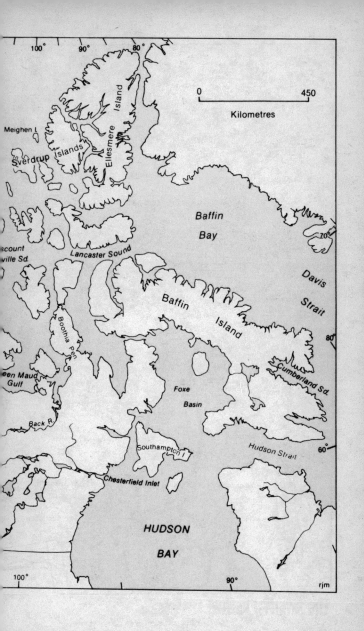

The Modern North

Introduction: Approaching the North

Canadians can no longer ignore the north. Over the past decade, a variety of issues and interest groups combined to keep northern affairs on the nation's agenda. The controversies are many, the emotions aroused often intense. The debates have raged without the antagonists having sufficient appreciation of the past, without an awareness of how the contemporary controversies affecting Canada's colonies represent a continuation of entrenched attitudes and positions.

The term "colonies" is used deliberately. So long a colony itself, Canada is most reluctant to acknowledge its own colonial tradition. Yet constitutional authority over the vast expanses of the Yukon and Northwest Territories rests in Ottawa, physically thousands of kilometers distant, and psychologically even further removed. To most northern residents the political realities are only too evident. The extensive powers of the national bureaucracy, the continued reliance on federal subsidies, and frequent federal intervention in regional affairs all make plain the north's colonial status. Recent constitutional improvements, including the establishment of cabinet-style governments and the selection of ''government leaders'' (a northern euphemism for premier), have only partially satisfied demands for greater local control. In the 1980s, northern politicians find themselves in the anachronistic position of refighting battles waged and eventually won by prairie politicians over half a century ago.

The prairies successfully challenged their inferior status. Alberta and Saskatchewan gained political autonomy in 1905, although they remained provinces unlike most others in that they did not have control over their public lands. The federal government relinquished control only in 1930, after the prairies' natural resources had been used to serve national objectives. Western leaders did not sit back quietly to enjoy their newfound constitutional equality. They remained resentful of past attempts at central Canadian control and manipulation and, after the post-World War II resource boom, took advantage of their unprecedented economic clout to issue a challenge to the eastern Canadian interpretation of Confederation.

The north's challenge to its colonial position has been markedly different. Subject to economic and social instability and all but ignored by the south, the territories have made only a few attempts over the years to redress the political imbalance. That changed in the 1970s. Northern issues became national issues, no longer minor antagonisms to be handled in bureaucratic solitude. The territories acknowledged their newfound importance by demanding a fairer constitutional arrangement. Southern interest in northern affairs has subsequently waned, though the proliferation of interest groups active on northern issues promises to keep these matters on the national agenda.

The southern neglect of the north is, to a certain extent, understandable. Despite its resource potential and enormous size, the region is sparsely populated. Together, the 482,515 km^2 of the Yukon and the 2,005,500 km^2 of the Northwest Territories comprise about one third of Canada's total area. With populations of 23,000 and 46,000 respectively, the territories scarcely equal the size of a modest southern city. This vast region is represented in the 282-member federal House of Commons by just three MPs: one for the Yukon and two for the Northwest Territories.

Many of the problems faced by the Yukon and Northwest Territories are, of course, shared by the people who inhabit the northern reaches of various provinces. The areas outside the settlement belt have been poorly served by governments, often neglected by business, and subject to the instability of boom-and-bust economies. The history of Labrador, "Nouveau Québec," northern Ontario, the non-agricultural sections of the prairie provinces and northern British Columbia have much in common with the experience "north of 60." The territories, though, suffer the further difficulty of being shackled by Canada's colonial system. The distinction is an important one, for the history of Canada's colonial north follows a very different constitutional and political path from that of the provincial "norths." For this reason our definition of north is the Yukon and Northwest Territories.

This book, then, is an historical view from the north, a northerner's perspective on his region. Inevitably, it is also an assessment of the place this fascinating region has held within the broader national context.

The northern experience imposes strong analytical temptations. Foremost among these is the urge to launch into a diatribe against injustices perpetrated on a constitutionally inferior region by the more powerful south — and hence to describe the pattern of northern history as one of systematic underdevelopment. Evidence exists to support the notion that, as colonies, the territories have been developed according to the needs of the south and that native and non-native northerners have had little say in their region's evolution. But this perspective suggests far more continuity in southern minds than in fact exists. The development of Canada's north has been anything *but* systematic, its only continuity provided by almost constant southern ignorance of northern issues. Neglect — not a conscious plan of underdevelopment — has characterized southern response to the Canadian North.

There have been brief exceptions. The discovery of gold in the Yukon River valley in the mid-1890s, the touting of the region's strategic significance during World War II, and more recently, a renewed search for oil and minerals, all awakened interest in the northern territories. Were it not for these short interludes when northern resources seemed of immediate benefit to the south, the region would have almost no place in the national conciousness.

This sporadic attention, which had wide-ranging implications for the evolution of the northern colonies, rests on simple foundations. Despite pious claims to their special status as citizens of a "Northern Nation," the Canadian people have shied away from their northlands. A few hardy promoter-adventurers like Vilhjalmur Stefansson and Farley Mowat have been drawn to the northern environment and, upon returning south, have popularized their visions of the region. Such visionaries, more romantics than pragmatists, remain propagators of an ideal that Canadians pay homage to, then consciously reject.

Canadians exhibit a curious lack of faith in the land that supposedly informs their character, demonstrating a continuing fear of frozen isolation that has shaped the pattern of development. Few non-natives have been content to remain in the north, whether they came during the early days of the mining frontier, as workers on an Arctic whaling vessel, to help build World War II defence projects or to grab a few quick dollars on contemporary oil rigs. They did not come north to make a home or to improve the region. Instead, each group has viewed the environment as an obstacle interfering with the productive harvesting of natural resources. The primary goal was to make money, often with little regard for the region, its people or its future. There is little difference (except in the workers' standard of living) between the whaling crews who huddled in their wooden ships off Herschel Island in the 1890s, waiting for the ice to break so they could return to San Francisco, and contemporary oil exploration crews, who live cloistered in mobile camps, are pampered with extravagant southern comforts, and fly south regularly on furlough.

Political and constitutional arrangements also perpetuated the north's difficulties. The territories lacked the political or economic resources to defend their interests adequately. Local governments, such as they were, depended on meagre federal grants. Even then, ultimate authority in both the Yukon and Northwest Territories rested with federal bureaucrats and appointees. There have been some improvements in recent times, as the federal government awarded greater local control to the territorial governments and adopted a more serious stance toward native land claims.

The historical experience of the Yukon and Northwest Territories should sound a warning. The federal government's continued hesitation over northern matters has been graphically demonstrated in the distressingly weak response to the voyage of the American vessel, *Polar Sea*, through Canadian territorial waters in the summer of 1985. Although the country's sovereignty over the vital northwest passage was at risk, fear of upsetting the United States seemingly overrode concern for the north. It was a replay of a familiar story.

The fact that territorial officials have gradually been granted increased powers, and now find themselves party to many federal-provincial discussions, and that native leaders from the north participate in heavily publicized constitutional conferences has not provided any guarantee of greater regional control. This colonial structure, founded on an inequitable constitutional, political and economic base, has institutionalized the unstable development of the Yukon and Northwest Territories. This relationship — between the colony and the colonizer — is the central concern of what follows.

1
The Land, Original Peoples and First Contacts

Robert Service spoke of the "Spell of the Yukon." Many others have written volumes on the north's effects on human intruders, particularly whites. All agree that the Canadian north exerts a powerful influence on those who inhabit, explore, or contemplate its vast reaches.

To many, the region assumes almost mystical proportions, growing beyond its political status or geography to become a state of mind. Because it is a land of physical extremes, of gloriously long summer days and painfully lengthy winter nights, the north elicits extreme responses. Many, shackled by the distances and the sameness of its horizons, are overwhelmed by the minuteness of their human intrusion. Others see opportunity. The north offers many natural wonders for those who can shrug off the isolation, or perhaps who seek the freedom distance provides in moving beyond the oases of southern comforts provided in the small northern communities.

While the land exacts very different responses from those who move north, the region has had difficulty shedding its singular image. Perhaps the strongest component of that image is the sense that the north consists of a single landscape. The solitary Inuit crossing an unbroken icy expanse, the light grey haze of the winter sky all but indistinguishable from the snow-covered land and sea, has come to symbolize the Canadian North. Now there are intruders — oil exploration rigs on artificial islands — but their perpendicular girders only reinforce the horizontal nature of the environment. Such images, focusing on tundra and ocean ice, fail to portray the great diversity in the Yukon and Northwest Territories.

There are three major regions within the north: the Yukon River basin, the Mackenzie River lowlands, and the Arctic slope which includes the vast archipelago reaching toward the pole.

The Yukon Territory is the most distinctive region. The territory's formal boundaries are defined in part by mountain barriers. To the southwest, the majestic St. Elias mountain range demarcates the border between the Yukon and Alaska. The centre is dominated by the massive Yukon Plateau, a heavily mineralized, undulating landscape carved into sections by the tentacles of the Yukon River system. This slow-flowing river drains most of the territory through its major tributaries, the Porcupine, Teslin, White, Stewart, and Pelly Rivers. To the east, the Yukon Plateau rises to join the Richardson, Selwyn and Mackenzie Mountains, which together form the divide between the north's two great rivers. Sections of the Yukon actually drain into the Mackenzie River system: to the southwest, the Frances River joins the treacherous Liard, while far to the north the Peel River bisects the Yukon, flowing to the northeast to join the Mackenzie shortly before the latter empties into the Arctic ocean.

Whereas streams, lakes, and mountains divide the Yukon, the Mackenzie lowlands are characterized by uniformity. The lowlands are an extension of the Great Plains. The vast land mass drained by the Mackenzie River consists of a myriad of rivers and lakes, and low, rolling hills carpeted with stunted trees. The

Mackenzie River and the equally impressive Great Bear and Great Slave Lakes dominate the region and, much as the Yukon River has done, shape the pattern of human activity. This is particularly true in the extreme north, where the broken estuary of the Mackenzie Delta joins the Arctic Ocean.

To the east and north, the tundra plains of the eastern Arctic stretch over seemingly endless distances. This segment, part of the massive Canadian Shield, is comparatively flat, pock-marked by minor depressions, many of which have trapped water to form a quiltwork of small lakes, adjoining streams, and a few turbulent waterways like the Back River. The treeless, barren landscape holds little vegetation and is dominated by the grey, bleak exposed rock surface of the Shield. The Arctic islands, stretching hundreds of miles northward from the continental coastline, stand separate. Though most of these islands are bleak and undistinguished, several, such as Baffin Island and the Queen Elizabeth Islands, are noted for their dramatic shapes and sharp mountain peaks. Together, the tundra and islands form a chilling landscape, largely devoid of soil, and sparsely populated.

Climatic and vegetation patterns generally follow the geographic formations. The treeless tundra, with its all but impassable muskeg, sharp winds, and extremely cold temperatures, offers few attractions for those conditioned by southern climes. The Mackenzie and Yukon River valleys are more accommodating, although scant rainfall and a short growing season restrict vegetation. Temperatures are, if anything, colder than in the east, since the river valleys act as catch basins for freezing air that can drop as low as -70° (F). Though winters last longer than in the south (and daily temperatures hit depths seldom experienced even on the prairies), the southern Yukon has its cold spells broken by occasional chinooks. These bursts of warm Pacific air forced over the coastal mountains generate a quick warming trend that can moderate temperatures by forty or fifty degrees. The winters, more debilitating for their length than their severity, are offset somewhat by the short but delightfully intense summers lit by the famous midnight sun.

The human history of the Canadian North has been shaped by the environment, and by the attempts of natives and Europeans to adapt to its harsh realities and exploit its many resources. For the white population, the attempt consisted primarily of overcoming climate, isolation, and geography, to recreate, as it were, the south in a northern setting. For the natives, the situation was the reverse. The land was not a foreign environment to be avoided or conquered; it was instead their universe, a constellation of physical and spiritual elements that defined their existence.

Pre-Contact Native Life

The contours of native adaptation to their home environment are central to any understanding of the history of the Canadian north. Their unity with the land and their reliance on the harvesting of natural resources conditioned the natives' response to the advance of Europeans into the north. Assessments of native lifestyle must be made carefully. There has been a tendency to impose non-native, southern, and middle-class values on the natives' way of life, which is typically expressed in descriptions of their standard of living as ''marginal'' and ''bare subsistence.'' The materialistic and acquisitive tendencies that dominate contemporary white Canadian society provide an extremely weak benchmark for the study of other cultures. It seems better to seek an understanding of other peoples on their own terms.

Anthropologist Marshall Sahlins challenged widely held perceptions of subsistence hunter-gatherers when he called them the ''original affluent society.'' To describe nomadic natives who satisfy basic human needs by following a pattern of seasonal mobility as ''affluent'' demands a redefinition of the term. Native peoples throughout the north altered their yearly cycles, their modes of harvesting, and material needs to suit their environment. The natives developed modest needs for accumulated property, and instead directed their energies toward fulfilling biological and cultural requirements. Thus, the harvesters became ''affluent'' according to their own standards. They placed value on leisure and travel rather than property, and provided for food and clothing requirements with comparative ease.

Though this concept seems acceptable for native societies in moderate climates, like the southern plains or the Pacific coast, it appears rather incongruous when applied to the Dene and Inuit of the Canadian North. The typical ungenerous portrait painted of the region's resources lends weight to assumptions of untold hardships in the perpetual drive to meet basic human needs, and supports the idea of societies living on the bare margins of subsistence. The natives did remain vulnerable to climatic problems, occasional food shortages, and a need to control population levels. It was also a lifestyle subject to change, and significant alterations followed the arrival of Europeans. Simply put, the natives recognized the positive aspects of their life even more than the Europeans disdained its mobility and irregularity. These cultural norms would obviously influence subsequent contact.

The northern natives' material culture naturally fell considerably short of that of the richer societies in southern settings. Because they lived in gentler climates, and shared in a richer and more diverse natural bounty, the Indians of the Pacific coast, the southern plains or the Great Lakes woodland followed a very different path of economic and cultural development.

Recent archaeological research in the northern Yukon has challenged long-standing interpretations of the prehistory of North America. Although there is general agreement that early man crossed to this continent from Siberia by way of a land bridge now submerged under the Bering Strait, scholars disagree as to the timing of that migration. Archaeological digs in the Porcupine River district suggest that the first inhabitants arrived some 27,000 years ago, though a few investigators speculate that it was much earlier. Those working in more geologically stable formations than those found in the northern Yukon argue that tool evidence indicates a likely arrival time of between 9500 and 7500 B.C.

These early peoples did not immediately disperse to the south and east. Much of the Yukon and central Alaska was not covered during the last ice age, which ended about 8000 B.C. People were able to inhabit the land, but could not move further until the ice receded. As the ice sheet retreated northward, the inhabitants gradually moved into the vacated lands and eventually across North and South America. The ending of the ice age also eliminated the bridge between this continent and Asia. The emergence of the Bering Strait as a water barrier slowed, but did not stop, the migration. Significant numbers of early harvesters continued to follow as late as 2000 B.C. By this time, the basic contours of regional native life were established, though all the societies would continue to adapt and change. The contact between the northern peoples of the two continents would continue, though late arrivals found it rather more difficult to move into the new land.

Centuries would pass between these first arrivals and European explorers. During the intervening generations, the inhabitants of the sub-Arctic and Arctic regions developed a culture closely attuned to their environment. In the forested districts, the Dene — or Athapaskans — developed. On the northern tundra, the Inuit emerged as a particularly distinctive people.

Numerous anthropological studies of the Dene people have provided extensive details on the differences between the native bands and tribes. There are, nonetheless, a large number of common features which tied the groups together. The Kutchin, Tutchone, Hare, Slave, Dogrib, Chipewyan, and others who inhabited what are now the Yukon and Northwest Territories were, anthropologist James VanStone suggests, "a cultural continuum carried on by a series of interlocking groups whose individual life ways differed only in minor details from those of their most immediate neighbours." The central characteristic of this "cultural continuum" was the ability to adapt socially and economically to specific local conditions (a situation which also explains the differences between the groups).

It is impossible to make a specific determination of the size and density of pre-contact native population. For many years, scholars believed that the native population of the Canadian North was extremely small, an assumption that fit their assessment of marginal prospects for life in the sub-Arctic. Kroeber's suggestion that a population density of less than one person per 100 km² was generally accepted without much question. Recent studies challenge that assessment. The anthropologist Shepherd Krech III examined population statistics for the Kutchin Indians and came up with a population density of almost twice the original estimate. According to Kroeber's estimate, the pre-contact (c. 1830) population of the Yukon would have been 4,700 people; Krech's statistics suggested more than 9,000 people inhabited the region. (The numbers are of course approximate, but suggest the substantial size of the pre-contact habitation of the sub-Arctic.)

Yukon Indians followed a highly nomadic seasonal cycle. They remained in the river valleys for much of the year, moving to the higher country only in pursuit of big game. Band movements depended primarily on the availability of major food supplies, such as migrating caribou herds and salmon runs along the Yukon and Alsek Rivers. The fish harvests, involving both salmon and land-locked species such as lake trout and whitefish, were particularly important. The natives would congregate each year, in the spring, at their fishing site. While the salmon run lasted, they would catch, dry, and smoke the fish, caching much of it for consumption later in the year.

Because the Yukon River valley supported only a modest stock of the crucial big game animals, the large bands which gathered for the fishery could not remain together. Instead they broke up into smaller units, typically grouped into extended families, and moved to family or band hunting territories.

The lifestyle of the Indians of the Mackenzie River lowlands differed only slightly from the Yukon pattern. There was no salmon fishery, although non-migratory species formed a crucial part of the native diet. Like their counterparts to the west, the Dene in the Mackenzie drainage region depended heavily on their moose hunts. (The role of the moose in Dene life was much like that of the bison to the Indians of the southern plains. There was a use for virtually every part of the animal.) The meat and organs were eaten, antlers and bones were used as utensils and tools, and the skins were worked for clothing, footwear, and even boats. The moose did not, however, travel in large, easily accessible herds. Groups relying on moose had to move frequently, as sustained hunting pressure could quickly deplete the number of the large, ungainly creatures in a specific area. Not all the Dene relied so heavily on moose. Several of the lowland groups and the Kutchin of the northern Yukon counted on organized hunts of woodland and barren ground caribou for their main supplies.

The fish, moose, and caribou were typically supplemented with small game, birds, and wild berries, most of which were gathered by women and small children. The diet was not as reliable or widely available as this list might suggest, and hardships and starvation were not uncommon. But by moving frequently, breaking into small groups as supplies dictated, and utilizing the full range of available resources, the natives assured themselves of an acceptable supply of food in all but extreme cases.

The mobility demanded by a harvesting existence placed strict limits on the complexity of Dene society. The yearly gatherings at the fisheries served as the focus for an ill-formed social system that had limited internal significance. The contrast with the highly organized native societies of the Tlingit, Haida and others along the Pacific coast was striking. The sea-based natives had well-developed class systems, strong leadership traditions, and, because of their rich natural setting, they also had the leisure time necessary to develop artistic and technical skills. Environmental conditions in the life of a sub-Arctic harvester demanded a more flexible approach to social organization and leadership.

Though the individual bands gathered with some regularity, the actual band structure exerted comparatively little infuence. Mechanisms were developed to provide for group cohesion despite the natives' all-but-constant movement. The Dene had a very loose clan system based on matriarchal relationships. Band members were divided into either the Crow or the Raven group. Members within a division were forbidden to marry, but were expected to provide food and assistance to others of their kind regardless of band affiliation. This rough kinship system provided at least a basic form of internal organization and aided relationships between the various bands. The selection of leaders similarly accorded ample flexibility. Leadership was typically a prerogative of age, but different leaders were selected according to the matter at hand, be it trading, hunting, warfare, or ceremonial events.

In the latter case, the bands had a shaman, or medicine man, to whom fell the daunting task of interpreting the spiritual world. Though their general religious beliefs lacked rigidity or widespread coherence, the Dene were a highly spiritual people. The Indians held very personal interpretations of, and relationships with, the spiritual world, unlike the codified structures European missionaries were to offer. Each adult sought the support of a spirit helper, a personal guardian who helped the person understand and master the environment. The leaders chosen for the various group tasks were those who ''know something a little,'' or had special insights gleaned from their spiritual helper which enabled them to excel at a particular task.

The spirit helpers were of vital importance, for the Dene believed that spirits inhabited the entire natural world. All things, animate and inanimate, possessed spirits, and failure to understand and respect these spirits could prove fatal. Children were taught at an early age that the forests surrounding the camps were filled with evil spirits. As anthropologist Alice Kehoe describes it:

> Bush Men, ragged and unkempt, are said to lurk around camps and steal children and women. In the past, there was a real threat from raiders, but the Bush Man represents a more generalized threat felt to emanate from the forest, a locus of powers best managed by a cohesive social group. Tales of Bush Men thus serve to teach children, and remind adults, of the value of the community and the possibly fatal result of too much individual independence.

Dene spiritualism proved highly functional, shaping social behaviour, their interaction with the physical environment, and the pursuit of game.

The Dene had developed a series of social conventions which reflected their continuing interdependence with and their reliance on the natural world, with all its vagaries. These conventions carried over into intergroup relations as well, governing personal conduct during trade and warfare.

The natives established viable and extensive trade networks long before the Europeans approached the coasts of North America. Within the region, individual groups had ready access to surpluses of certain goods, but were deficient in others. The Kutchin in the northern Yukon were near huge herds of caribou, but lacked a supply of fish. The Tutchone in the south could collect copper, metal, and furs, which they traded for the dried fish, shell ornaments, and cedar bark baskets available from the Tlingit Indians, one of the coastal tribes. Trading usually occurred once a year, as one group travelled to meet another in a spring fishing camp. The Tlingit from the coast insisted on coming inland to trade, forbidding the interior Indians from using the closely-guarded mountain passes to the ocean. In the northern Yukon, the Kutchin often travelled to the Arctic Ocean to trade with the Inuit near Herschel Island.

The trade networks assumed considerable importance over time, and were adapted after the arrival of European traders to bring the highly desired manufactured goods into the interior. In several instances, special social conventions were developed to ensure that trade continued even during times of war. The Inuit and Kutchin, for example, forbade trading partners to harm each other, allowing the groups to exchange goods without interruption.

Such arrangements proved essential, for warfare and confrontations were not uncommon among the Dene. There were particular problems with native groups in neighbouring regions. The Dene near the Arctic coast had a running battle with the Inuit which often dissolved into damaging raids and bloody wars. The natives of the southern interior Yukon encountered similar problems with the militarily powerful Tlingit of the Pacific northwest coast.

Relations among Dene groups, and even more so between the Dene and other natives, were continually uneasy, buoyed by the need for trade but hampered by repeated raids and larger confrontations. The arrival of the Europeans would create further dissension, increasing the reliance on inter-tribal trade while straining already intense rivalries.

The Inuit

Historic Inuit culture evolved from three distinct periods of native habitation. The first, the Arctic Small Tool Tradition or Denbigh, spread from Siberia to Greenland around 2400 B.C., aided by the generally warmer temperatures of that epoch. As the weather cooled appreciably in the north, the people retreated southward, leaving much of the Arctic unoccupied. The Arctic Small Tool Tradition was succeeded by the Dorset culture, which flourished between 1000 B.C. and 1000 A.D. The Dorset were similar to the Inuit. They probably originated the snow-block igloo, though they also built sod houses. Their hunting technology contained several key adaptations. They made regular use of sleds, pulled by people rather than dogs, and made frequent use of shaped bone for implements and weapons. The Dorset were, in turn, replaced around 1000 A.D. by the Thule Culture, a whale-hunting society which migrated east from Alaska. The superior hunting technology of this new people, which included the use of dogsleds for land transportation, and umiaks and kayaks for ocean travel, permitted it to quickly absorb other Arctic groups as it spread rapidly along the Arctic coast, reaching as far as Greenland. This latest addition marked the final pre-contact migration into the region. A long cold spell in the seventeenth and eighteenth centuries and problems harvesting the whales which formed the basis of Thule subsistence forced a gradual modification in their culture. They turned increasingly to other game, especially seal and caribou, and gradually abandoned their stone and turf houses for tents and igloos. These modifications, complete by the early eighteenth century, represented the change from Thule to historic Inuit culture.

The Inuit adaptation to the harsh environment of the Canadian Arctic is truly remarkable. The land did not offer an abundance of resources, but by living in small, mobile communities that typically migrated between winter camps near the ocean and summer hunting camps inland, and by making specific changes in hunting patterns to suit local conditions the Inuit generated an acceptable living. Several cultural attributes were common to almost all Canadian Inuit groups. The kayak, a small skin boat, was used for ocean hunting. The igloo, or snowhouse, was the common form of winter habitation, with most Inuit changing to skin tents during the summer. The Inuit also developed a set of clothing well suited to northern conditions, including waterproof boots and two-layer caribou skin outerwear. The stone kudlik, a lamp which provided light, heat and a place to cook, was also found throughout the Arctic.

Although the Inuit shared much in common, their need for an accommodation with the local environment required a number of regional adaptations. In the eastern barren lands, the Caribou Inuit had moved away from the coast and subsisted on the huge caribou herds which roamed the area. Their reliance on this single animal often left them very vulnerable to changes in migration patterns or shortages of game. Conversely, the Mackenzie Delta Inuit inhabited a relatively rich land, marked by an abundance of game, including caribou, musk-ox and moose, and plentiful sea resources, especially baleen and beluga whales. The concentration and variety of food resources allowed the Mackenzie Delta Inuit to congregate in larger numbers than was possible elsewhere in the Canadian Arctic. Seasonal groupings of up to 1,000 were not uncommon and substantial villages remained together year-round. The Netsikik people, who lived near King William Island, developed in a different fashion again. Here, seals provided the mainstay of their life, and the natives developed particular skills at hunting these animals, by kayak during the short season of open water and through air-holes in the ice in winter. There were yet other Inuit groups who similarly exploited those resources in greatest abundance in their homelands, and whose cultures therefore differed from the Inuit norm.

Inuit spiritual beliefs similarly followed a pattern of regional and individual variation. Like the Dene, the Inuit believed that the universe was controlled by numerous spirits. Animal spirits had to be respected and the mistreatment of game carried strong social and spiritual penalties. The various Inuit communities contained "doctors," who interpreted the spiritual world, healed the ill, and provided guidance for the hunts. The Inuit too believed that each person had a helping spirit, typically a bird or animal, which they could call on for help in times of trouble. Inuit spiritual beliefs were not formalized or overly complex, and left much room for individual interpretation and experience. Each group, however, developed a fairly rigid set of taboos designed to ensure that the spirits were not angered, and more generally, to provide a system of social control.

The Inuit believed in a close bond between the human and animal worlds. Keith Crowe, in his survey of northern native peoples, tells of a widely shared Inuit legend, "The girl who married a dog," which exemplifies this relationship:

> The most common Inuit version is about a girl called Uinagumasuituk, 'the girl who didn't want a husband.' Her father makes her marry a handsome stranger who is really a dog in disguise. Some of their children are human and they become Inuit. The others are like dogs and become the other human races. Later the girl is pushed from a boat by her father but she clings to the side. He cuts off her fingers, which become whales, seals and other sea creatures. She sinks down to become Sedna, Nuliajuq, or Takkanaaluk, the goddess of the sea.

Many Inuit tales and spiritual beliefs stressed the importance of maintaining a balance between human occupation and the natural world.

First Contact

The Dene and Inuit societies extant at the point of European contact represented the adaptations of countless generations to the specific opportunities and limitations of the northern environment. The coming of explorers and fur traders would obviously upset the native peoples' accommodation with their environment, but the Dene and Inuit were by no means defenseless.

By the time the first Europeans reached the Canadian North in the late sixteenth century, the Dene and Inuit had inhabited the land for thousands of years. It had not been easy, and hardship and starvation were not unknown. The natives had discovered the dangers of over consumption and the need to husband the harvestable game of the northland. The centuries of exclusively native habitation passed without appreciable environmental damage, a striking contrast to the destructive effects that accompanied the comparatively brief period of European occupation of the Canadian North.

The Europeans had little but disdain for the pre-industrial, stone-age societies they encountered in the north, and would find in their own metal products, manufactured goods and acquisitive values sufficient justification for their sense of superiority over the native inhabitants. They also soon found that their material wealth and "civilized" society would provide little protection against the natural conditions of the Arctic and sub-Arctic.

The meeting of Europeans and natives proved to be more equal than the Europeans initially anticipated. They often came to rely on native technology or knowledge in order to survive. The natives themselves saw opportunity in the arrival of the Europeans. They quickly identified the value of metal implements and other goods brought by explorers and traders, and responded to the advance of the white men out of self-interest, rather than fear or awe. They remained confident in their way of life, and so addressed the opportunities posed by the arrival of explorers, fur traders and miners from a position of some strength. The meeting of cultures would eventually bring new economic systems, disease, alcohol, and eventually government control, but the problems inherent in the introduction of these elements would emerge rather more slowly.

Initial contact was modest and tentative. European explorers hoping to uncover a route to the Orient across the top of North America began to probe the northern reaches of the continental land mass. The European exploration of Canada's vast sub-Arctic and Arctic regions carried all the elements of the classic adventure tale. Men repeatedly exposed themselves to an unknown land, searching for fame and fortune in the mysterious and threatening north, facing dangers and suffering that would cripple the less hardy. The individual stories provide Canada with a roll-call of adventurers that would do any country proud. Yet the explorers are rather peripheral to the social and economic history of the north. They came to fill in glaring holes on the maps of the northern hemisphere, to satisfy scientific curiosities about the frozen northland, or to gain the rewards guaranteed to those who solved the mystery of the northwest passage. Explorers like Baffin, Foxe, James, and Jens Munk, who together defined the contours of Hudson Bay and the eastern Arctic islands; and those like Franklin, Back, Richardson, Simpson, and Dease who examined the central Arctic, all played a vital role in redefining European perceptions of the north.

The explorers provided a rather singular image of the northland to their southern and European audiences. Their writings were eloquent and evocative, describing with true passion the natural wonders which they faced and, often with classic understatement, the hardships they encountered. Though the explorers were clearly emphasizing the Arctic portions of their travels, their descriptions were often sufficiently vague as to suggest they covered the entire western part of British North America. These explorers' memoirs consequently tarred the entire western and northern regions with the same description. The image they projected of a frigid, barren wasteland proved hard to shake, even for the more temperate zones to the south.

Several examples illustrate the contradictory images projected of the north. John Richardson provided an appealing portrait of the region when he wrote in 1849:

> The sun in the clear spring atmosphere has a power which equals that of the tropics, and although there is a great difference between the temperature of the air here and at the Equator, yet the direct rays of the sun act with greater force on the skin in Rupert's Land. When the snow is filled with water it looks like frosted silver in the sunlight, and every little rising is studded with innumerable polished facets, as if sprinkled with diamonds. The intensity of all this splendour soon becomes painful to the eye.

Such visages were quickly forgotten when followed with pages and books describing the less attractive aspects of life in the north. Edward Parry's 1824 description typified this southern response:

> When once the earth is covered, all is monotonous whiteness — not merely for days and weeks, but for more than half a year together. Whichever way the eye is turned, it meets a picture calculated to impress upon the mind an idea of inanimate stillness, of that motionless stupour with which our feelings have nothing congenial; of anything, in short, but life. In the very silence there is a deadness with which a human spectator appears out of keeping.

After the early voyages, it soon became evident that the northwest passage, if ever found, would be so long and through such forbidding waters that it could never be economical. But still the explorers came. The search became more purely scientific, spurred on by a reward offered by the British government for the first ship to navigate the passage. This effort, which cost thousands of dollars and took dozens of lives before it was completed, actually left little mark on the region itself. The explorers were obviously transient, passing through as quickly as possible, and making few contacts with the native people. The Europeans' contributions consisted of improved maps, lessons in what materials and techniques would and would not work in the Arctic, and eloquent tales of their adventures, all of which found a ready market in the south and in Europe, but had little effect in the north.

The story of Arctic exploration has been often and well told. From Martin Frobisher in the sixteenth century to Roald Amundsen in the twentieth, men have battled with the elements and the limits of their knowledge in an attempt to breach the impressive barrier of Arctic ice and rock. Two episodes, the voyages of Martin Frobisher and John Franklin's ill-fated expedition of 1845, illustrate the expectations, implications, and values which dominated these attempts to uncover the secrets of the Arctic.

The three voyages of Martin Frobisher unexpectedly linked the search for the northwest passage with the prospect of mineral wealth. Frobisher first travelled west from England in 1576, carrying instructions to seek a route to Cathay over the top of the newly discovered continent of North America. Less formally, he also carried dreams of the sort of great riches that the Spanish and Portuguese had discovered in Central America.

Frobisher was something of a rogue, a one-time privateer who brought unquestioned courage and determination to the formidable task before him. He sailed his bark *Gabriel* to the northwest, reached land and discovered a promising ''strait'' (actually the modern

Frobisher Bay). Frobisher did not have a chance to test his new discovery. While sailing along the waterway, later shown to be a bay, Frobisher's ship came upon a number of Inuit. After a brief trading ceremony, which indicated that the Inuit had dealt with Europeans before, Frobisher arranged to have the natives guide him further. He soon regretted his decision, for the Inuit captured five of his men, then retreated. Attempts to secure their release failed. Frobisher decided to return home, stopping first to pick up rock samples before setting sail for England.

The unscheduled stop proved fortuitous, or so Frobisher must have thought. The first two men to assay the rock in England wrote it off as worthless iron pyrite; but a third (who may have been bribed) claimed it was gold. Word spread rapidly. Frobisher had discovered gold! Plans were quickly put in place for a return voyage. There were two reasons to return forthwith — the possiblity of finding gold and Frobisher's suggestion that he may have discovered a route to Cathay. The explorer and his supporters applied for and received a royal charter to "Meta Incognito," making it much easier for the promoters to raise money. Frobisher left again in 1577, his three ships filled with sailors, soldiers (in case the Inuit were met again), miners, and the necessary supplies.

The voyage proceeded according to plan, and the miners were put to work on several promising sites. Frobisher tried to find the five men left behind the previous year, but his efforts resulted only in a pitched battle with the Inuit, which left him with several captives and an arrow wound in his buttocks. He returned to England, convinced that the northland had few prospects except ore, with which he had filled the holds of his ships. The ore was taken again to assayers and refiners, who confirmed the exciting, but incorrect, news that the ore was rich in gold. The seemingly profitable return convinced the Cathay Company to outfit a third expedition to Frobisher's Strait.

Frobisher carried the expectations of Queen and country when he set sail again in 1578, this time leading an expedition of fifteen ships and enough supplies to provide for a winter settlement at Meta Incognito. Though he lost several ships on the voyage, Frobisher brought his convoy through to the mine site. Again miners were set to work at various sites along the bay, and Frobisher himself sailed on further, hoping to unlock the mysteries of the "strait." Short on supplies and facing resistance from the miners slated to be left in the north, Frobisher decided to pull out and return to England.

The episode ended ingloriously. The attempts to find a refiner who could extract gold from iron pyrites continued for five years. Finally, as a historian noted shortly thereafter, "when neither Gold, Silver, nor any metall could be drawne [from them] we saw them thrown away to repayre the high-wayes." The Cathay Company faced heavy debt and challenges from shareholders and creditors. Frobisher's reputation, which had ranked with the leading explorers of his age, plummeted as he and his associates were accused of misleading investors and the public. It was an ignominious end to a glorious enterprise, and it did a great deal to sour the English on the commercial prospects of the north. Though the behaviour of the Inuit suggested that they had previously encountered Europeans (probably fishermen heading for Newfoundland), the confrontation with Frobisher's men provided a poor starting point for subsequent relations. The European effort, emanating for the most part from

England, turned to the search for the northwest passage. John Davis' explorations in the area west of Greenland, Henry Hudson's discovery of Hudson Bay in 1610, and the subsequent surveys by Baffin, Bylot, James, and others quickly demonstrated that there was no quick or obvious route to the Orient.

The realization that the northwest passage might not exist, or that if it did it would not prove viable, was hard to accept. The search lost its economic imperative and turned into an academic pursuit. After decades of neglect, during which time exploratory efforts concentrated on the southern fur trading districts, a second major thrust to uncover the secrets of the high Arctic came in the nineteenth century. The British government's offer of a cash reward for the first to sail through the passage added to increasing scientific interest in the area.

The British explorers tended to reject native means of travel and dress, often to their own distress. Partly because they were sea-farers, and partly because they held to the imperious British worldview, they clung tenaciously to their own methods of investigation, outfitting, provisioning and travel. Although these methods had often stood their countrymen in good stead in other parts of the globe, they proved less than satisfactory in the north. Lessons were learned. The standard practice of ship-borne exploration was gradually combined with ''light party'' expeditions, whereby a group would leave the ice-bound ship and travel by sledge, living off the land where possible to broaden out the search.

John Franklin stood at the head of this nineteenth-century exploratory corps, his early discoveries and subsequent catastrophic failure providing much of the impetus for continued surveys of the Arctic. Franklin's northern career began in 1819, when he led a lengthy, and almost disastrous exploration of the coastline east of the Coppermine River. By travelling in smaller boats and travelling overland, Franklin had added a great deal to existing knowledge of the Arctic coast. He returned in 1825, this time to chart the as yet unknown portions of the coastline. Franklin headed west from the mouth of the Mackenzie, but he was forced to turn back by deteriorating weather. Although Franklin had established impressive credentials as a northern explorer, his early efforts had demonstrated the dangers of travel in the Arctic.

John Franklin returned to the Arctic in 1845. In the intervening years, a series of voyages by John Ross, Thomas Simpson and Peter Warren Dease, George Back and Edward Parry had clarified the map of the Arctic islands. The successful navigation of the northwest passage finally seemed possible and John Franklin was selected to lead the official British Royal Navy expedition.

Franklin set out with two ships, the *Erbus* and *Terror*. Though the recent voyages of men like Simpson, Back and Rae had demonstrated the value of travelling light and living, at least in part, off the land, Franklin seemed determined to stay with his vessels, which had been outfitted with auxiliary steam power. He also packed enough supplies for a three-year voyage, which reduced his dependence on local resources but also made his crew vulnerable to scurvy. As historian Hugh Wallace has remarked: ''The ethos was to carry the home environment with the party and dominate the Arctic, rather than fit into and come to terms with the Arctic.''

This approach proved to be folly. The ships were locked in ice off King William Island, with Franklin waiting for the sea to clear so that he could push the ships through the remaining miles of the passage. The opportunity never came, food supplies ran short, and the ships had to be abandoned. Franklin and his entire crew perished, leaving scant clues as to their fate. The British launched a number of investigative expeditions, hoping to find Franklin or the remains of his expedition. Ships pushed through the ice from the east and west, and several groups came overland from the south. In their searching, these expeditions added even greater detail to the map of the Arctic islands and identified several additional "passages" through the ice-blocked archipelago. The fate of the Franklin crew remained unknown until 1854, when a team led by John Rae found evidence of the party's demise. By that year, the search for Franklin had grown to twenty-two naval expeditions and several land-based surveys. The final cost, according to one estimate, was £2,000,000. The British Admiralty's method of large, ship-based surveys had been shown to be impractical, but the British were reluctant to abandon their time-honoured approach. The loss of John Franklin and his crew became the price paid for ignoring the realities of travel and survival in the Canadian North.

Arctic exploration continued after the tremendous flurry of activity in the mid-nineteenth century. With the pursuit of the northwest passage finally laid to rest, the emphasis now shifted northward, to the as yet unknown lands of the archipelago. The British were joined by scientists and adventurers from the United States, Norway and Denmark. The internationalization of the high Arctic threatened the tenuous British hold on the region. They had little desire to formally assert their sovereignty, but did not want the area to fall into foreign hands. To head off any such claims, the British government formally transferred jurisdiction for the Arctic islands to the Canadian government in 1880.

Scientific surveys, exploration and simple adventuring continued on this most mysterious of the world's remaining frontiers. These explorations, from the early search for the northwest passage through to the expeditions at the turn of the century, were largely peripheral to regional developments. They held considerable interest to external spectators, particularly those in geographical and scientific societies in Europe, the United States and Canada. The surveys and cartographic exercises provided the maps which opened the way for future development. Perhaps of greatest importance, the explorers' journals and reports helped create and reinforce external images of what one book called *The Frozen Zone*. While their descriptions of the north as cold and inhospitable may have been apt for the Arctic islands, the image thus projected was quickly and incorrectly applied to the entire northwest beyond the limits of white settlement. The explorers had not, therefore, opened the north, though their discoveries certainly provided a possible path. That task fell to the fur traders, who conducted separate explorations from the south.

2
The Early Fur Trade

Until the arrival of European fur traders in the Canadian North, the region lacked economic value to colonizing powers and therefore attracted only marginal interest. When the fur trade arrived, it brought the Dene into the European economic system, and gave them access to new technology and material wealth. The advance of the fur trade also brought hitherto unknown diseases and a new constellation of social relations. The trade was not as narrowly exploitative as historians have long argued, for the natives played a very influential role in fur trade relations. Once the fur traders arrived, however, the old Dene order was irrevocably changed and a substantial re-ordering of Indian social and economic life followed. The story must begin with the Europeans and their efforts to incorporate the north into their fur trading empires.

Expansion of the Fur Trade

The Hudson's Bay Company (HBC) was issued a formal charter in 1670, granting it a legal commercial monopoly over Rupert's Land, all the land draining into Hudson Bay. From the beginning, however, the firm faced serious competition from French fur traders working out of Montreal. The rivalry forced an intense battle for the trade and spurred further expansion into the northwest. Pushing back the fur trading frontier proved to be a slow process, impeded by high costs, vast distances, and the difficulties of extended over-land travel through unfamiliar terrain.

The HBC, for many years the smaller of the two branches of the fur trade, seldom strayed from its "sleep by the frozen sea." The company did send a few men inland, largely to make contact with Indian traders, but the tragic end to a 1719 expedition searching for copper deposits along the northwest coast of Hudson Bay was sufficient to postpone for more than half a century any further attempts to push northward. Samuel Hearne was selected to lead another expedition to the reported copper deposits, though he was sent overland rather than along the coast. His first two attempts failed, but aided by the Chipewyan leader Matonabee, he reached his objective in 1771. Hearne's group followed the Coppermine River to a point near its mouth where, to Hearne's horror, his Chipewyan companions attacked an Inuit camp, resulting in a savage massacre which soured relations between the native groups for generations. The copper deposits turned out to be of no value. The trip had some academic significance, however, for it indicated the northern extent of the continent, disproving theories still extant about mythical straits joining the Pacific and the Atlantic. As an economic venture, it had little impact and the HBC retreated to its less adventurous stance in the fur trade.

The Company was soon forced to move. The British conquest of New France in 1760 resulted in the rapid reorganization of the fur trade in the northwest. The HBC initially believed that the transfer would confirm its legal monopoly, only to have Scottish and American entrepreneurs link up with the remaining French-Canadian traders to revitalize the Montreal trade. The high costs of transportation and competition weakened the independent traders, convincing several to join with

Montreal merchants to form the loosely-structured North West Company. That organization collapsed due to internal tensions, only to be reborn in a slightly different form in 1779.

Though the two firms did not have the field entirely to themselves, by the late 1790s competition centred on the aggressive North West Company and the less active HBC. With its profits slashed by the Montreal firm's thrusts into the heart of HBC trading territories, the London-based "monopoly" had no choice but to follow the competition inland. The resulting rivalry proved intense, bitter and even violent. Both firms disbursed generous quantities of alcohol to the Indians, set up posts near their rival's, and resorted to ambushes and kidnapping in increasingly desperate attempts to undermine their opponents. Fur prices rose as native traders played the competitors off each other, and other expenses skyrocketed as the firms opened too many posts and hired too many men. As the battle intensified, the trading companies looked west and north for fur reserves as yet untouched by competition. Out of this battle for the trade of the northern plains came the push into the Mackenzie River valley.

The fur traders moved onto the frontier in rather different fashion than the scientific explorers of the high Arctic. Often with years of experience in the northwest, the traders were well trained at living off the land. They also travelled with native or mixed blood guides and labourers, whose skills further enhanced the explorers' ability to advance into unfamiliar territory. The fur traders came with less grandiose ambitions than did their counterparts further north. They sought to open new trading territories and to locate cheaper supply routes; any benefit to geographic knowledge was clearly secondary.

The Montreal traders, who were attempting to outflank the HBC and overcome internal competition, led the advance. A cutthroat adventurer named Peter Pond provided the key discovery. In 1779, he located the Methy Portage, a 12-mile hike over the height of land separating the Hudson Bay and Mackenzie River drainage basins. This opened up vast new tracts of trading territory in the Athabaska country, certainly the richest remaining fur preserve in North America.

The HBC proved to be less complacent than expected, and attempted, after a fashion, to follow the North West Company as it expanded. This in turn forced the Montreal traders to push on again, hoping that further discoveries would provide either a cheap transportation route to the Pacific (thus freeing the company from its arduous and costly overland trek back to Montreal) or another rich fur reserve.

The task of formal exploration fell to Alexander Mackenzie. By the 1780s, the North West Company had reached Great Slave Lake, but had not yet traced the watershed it opened up to its expected point of discharge in the Pacific Ocean. Mackenzie set out on the river draining Great Slave Lake in 1789, only to find that its placid but lengthy path led to the Arctic Ocean. He dubbed his discovery the "River of Disappointment." In 1793 Mackenzie tried once more to find a viable route to the Pacific. He charted a path, but one that clearly had little potential as a fur trade supply route. The route to the north — the Mackenzie River — would, in the long run, prove to be more important to the fur trade.

The North West Company was reluctant to head north, for the distances involved imposed heavy costs. But the lure of untapped resources proved irresistible in the end, particularly as the battle for dwindling stocks in the south escalated. The North West Company tried first in 1796, opening a post at the mouth of Great Slave Lake. A native attack thwarted this first attempt, but the company persisted. An unexpected challenge from Alexander Mackenzie's short-lived XY Company (1800-1805) forced the North West Company to press on. The merger of the two firms in 1805 allowed for a consolidation of the trade. Several posts were closed, leaving only the major establishments at Fort Norman, Fort Good Hope and the "Forks" (of the Mackenzie and Liard Rivers). From this solid base, the company undertook a modest expansion along the Liard River.

The prohibitively high costs of trading in this isolated region, coupled with resistance from the natives who protested the less generous conditions of trade after competition ended, forced the North West Company to abandon the district for a year in 1815. By now, both the North West Company and the HBC were reeling from the financial ill-effects of competition. In 1820, continued losses on both sides forced the long-time combatants to the bargaining table. A merger followed the next year. Freed from the burdens of competition, the reconstituted Hudson's Bay Company turned its attentions toward revitalizing the western and northern trades. Newly-arrived George Simpson was given the task of bringing order, efficiency and harmony to the still bitterly divided fur trading corps. The "Little Emperor," as he was less than affectionately known, brought peace and financial order to the company's affairs. He did so with ruthless determination, imposing strict conservation measures in over-trapped areas, laying off many employees, slashing salaries, closing posts, and adopting strong competitive practices whenever and wherever the HBC's trade was threatened. Simpson also began an orderly expansion to the northwest, for he believed that these as yet unexploited districts held great potential.

The timing and direction of HBC expansion were partially dictated by the activities of the Russian American Fur Company. Years of intense competition along the Pacific northwest coast had ended with the Anglo-Russian convention of 1825. The accord granted Russia formal ownership of the Alaskan panhandle and the entire Alaskan peninsula west of the 141st Meridian. Through the Russian American Fur Company, the Russians consolidated their hold on the northern coastal trade and, to the chagrin of Simpson and the HBC, tapped the lucrative land-based trade as well.

The HBC advanced with two objectives: to meet the Russian challenge and to identify potential fur trading districts in the as yet unknown northwest. Governor Simpson's fears intensified after 1837 when Russian traders at the mouth of the Stikine River repulsed efforts by Company officer Peter Skeene Ogden to establish a post upstream, in British territory.

With the obvious ocean route blocked, the Hudson's Bay Company fell back to the overland route. Simpson's anger at this state of affairs was particularly evident in 1838, after he had learned of Odgen's difficulties and the failure of John Hutchinson to open a trail from the Liard River to the coast:

> The Governor and Committee consider it a stain upon the character of the concern that the Russians should so long be allowed to drain our Country of its riches which form the most valuable part of their trade and enable them to oppose us so vigorously on the North-West Coast while we remain paralyzed by terror in Mackenzie's [valley] through the childish reports of a timid nervous creature who was never calculated for the enterprising life of an Indian trader.

The company had known since John McLeod's exploration of 1831 that a river link existed between the Mackenzie district and the coastal watershed, and Simpson was determined to make use of it. After Hutchinson's failure to find it, Robert Campbell was dispatched to continue the exploration, though his effort also failed.

Campbell, anxious to continue as an explorer, a task he preferred to that of a fur trader, pleaded for permission to return. But the imperative for expansion had disappeared. Extensive negotiations between Governor Simpson and Russian American Fur Company counterpart, Baron Wrangell, led to the signing of a major accord in 1839. The HBC leased the continental portion of the Alaskan panhandle in return for 2,000 land otter skins per year, plus a promise to provide other supplies as required. The company could now collect the furs of the northwest along the coast, allowing the Tlingit Indians to trade with the inland natives and carry those furs down to company traders. The much more expensive option of trading for furs inland, then carrying the pelts across the continent to Hudson Bay could be abandoned. The impetus for further expansion to the northwest seemed, for the moment, to have stalled.

Expansion remained on hold until 1837. That year Thomas Simpson and Peter Warren Dease were exploring the Arctic coastline west of the Mackenzie River, completing a survey first undertaken by John Franklin in 1826. During the voyage, the explorers crossed the mouth of a new river, which they called the Colville. Simpson noted that ''The Colville separates the Franklin and Pelly Mountains, the last seen by us; and probably flows in a long course through a rich fur country, and unknown tribes, in the west side of the Rocky

Mountains.'' In short order, Governor Simpson had explorers probing the mountain barriers which sealed off this new district.

The task fell to two men. John Bell was sent to open Fort McPherson on lower Peel River and was directed to continue explorations to the west. In the south, Robert Campbell was directed to search the headwaters of the Liard River system for what the Indians called ''Toucho'' or Great Water, believed to be the Colville. Their respective paths proved most difficult. The eastern Kutchin repeatedly interfered with Bell's efforts because they feared that expansion would undermine their lucrative middleman position. Such problems with native opposition and the dangers of river travel along the tumultuous Liard slowed Campbell's advance.

Both men eventually found the ''great river,'' later shown to be the westward flowing ''Youcon'' (now Yukon) and not the northerly Colville. Campbell reached the Yukon basin first, in 1840. Bell finally breached the Richardson Mountains and reached the slow-moving Yukon River in 1845. The HBC quickly exploited their explorers' discoveries. In 1848, Campbell erected Fort Simpson at the forks of the Yukon and Pelly Rivers. The expansion from Peel River post proceeded more expeditiously. In 1847, only two years after Bell's initial voyage, Alexander Hunter Murray established Fort Youcon at the junction of the Yukon and Porcupine Rivers, a point they immediately recognized to be some distance outside British territory.

The HBC had, with notable speed, incorporated the far northwest into its trading empire. By 1850, the Mackenzie District had demonstrated its fur trade potential, although the time and cost involved in shipping furs and supplies across the continent cut sharply into profits. The potential of the newly opened Yukon region remained unknown, largely due to Campbell's numerous reversals in the south, but initial reports pointed to a profitable future. The nineteenth-century expansion of the HBC was more or less complete. The success of the company's early initiatives in the area demonstrated that the initial optimism had not been misplaced.

The Native Role

The fur trade has often been treated as a European-only episode in Canadian history. Library shelves are full with books on explorers, company officials, and business competition. Obviously the natives were important as hunters and trappers, but recent studies of the western Canadian fur trade have shed further light on their vital role in influencing the shape of fur trade economic and social relations. The natives were not passive participants in the trade.

The general contours of the northern fur trade after 1821 can be quickly sketched. The company trading posts were supplied each year by canoe brigades, which brought tons of food (mainly pemmican), trading goods and other supplies from the HBC main depot at York Factory.

Most of the Indians trading at the posts of the Mackenzie District (which included the Yukon establishments) came in once or twice a year. After a greeting ceremony, complete with gift exchanges, trading would commence. The posts were busy places only during the trading season, when there could be several hundred Indians encamped around the fort. In addition to the trading Indians, a number of "homeguard" or "post" Indians gathered more permanently around the trading post. These Indians often traded with other, more distant bands, preventing them from visiting the post if necessary to protect their position. They also hunted and fished for the company and, when required, could find work as guides or tripmen with the annual fur brigades.

The fur trade obviously had far-reaching implications for those natives involved. There is little question that the Indians welcomed the advance of the fur trade. They gained access to the technology and material devices of a different age and civilization, but they also faced the devastation caused by imported disease, a depletion of game through over-hunting, and considerable economic and social change. With the arrival of the fur trade the Dene pattern of life was disrupted, as new forces tied to distant market economies now dominated life in the north.

The natives in the north first sampled European material culture decades before explorers actually entered their lands. Pre-contact trading networks had long facilitated exchange in local products between groups and regions. When European traders arrived in the western interior and along the Pacific coast in the late eighteenth and early nineteenth centuries, these same networks brought the new trading goods into the north. Shaped flint knives and bone implements were readily discarded when forged iron knives and axes and metal pots came available. There was great demand for these new goods, and those natives with access to European traders found themselves in a strong trading position. Natives able to trade directly with the Europeans set themselves up as middlemen between the posts and distant Indian bands. The problems encountered by John Bell and Robert Campbell during their early exploration to the northwest can be traced largely to the fact that their planned expansion threatened existing middleman trading networks. Indeed, the emergence of the middleman forced a restructuring of inter-tribal trade networks and altered the balance of power among native groups in the region.

It was not the only change. The introduction of metal axes, knives, guns, and later steel traps enabled the hunters and trappers to work more efficiently than before (though that could easily lead to over-harvesting and a depletion of game). The trader's outfit contained a wide variety of goods he was only too anxious to sell to the natives. The Indians approached the new bounty with extreme caution. Goods of obvious benefit to the native lifestyle, like metal pots and steel knives, were quickly incorporated. Supplies of possible benefit, such as blankets, were tried on an almost experimental basis. The natives' needs and desires changed rather more gradually than is usually thought. Through the first decades trade was limited to essentials, including guns, knives, and pots, with a few "luxuries" like tobacco and shells (for decorative and ceremonial purposes), purchased only if furs remained once the essentials had been obtained.

The fur traders had requests of their own, and encouraged the natives to bring in more of the highly valued furs, principally beaver, marten, and fox. Such fur-bearers had been harvested in pre-contact times, but the arrival of the traders increased the intensity of the hunt exponentially. The Dene were still harvesters, but they placed an increasing importance on furs and proportionately less on meat. In many areas of Canada, pressure from the fur trade resulted in a decline in available fur stocks, although this occurred much later in the north than elsewhere. Diminishing hunts meant reduced packs of furs to trade, which could have, in turn, lessened pressure on the resources.

But the HBC was a commercial enterprise. It was therefore imperative that the natives be encouraged to continue hunting, even when harvests were skimpy. The HBC met this problem, and the difficulties encountered when facing competitive traders, by providing credit to post hunters. Goods were issued on account, with the firm hoping that this would encourage the hunters to exert themselves and to trade exclusively at the HBC posts. The trading system involved far more than a simple exchange of pelts for supplies. The combination of gift giving at the commencement of trading, credit, the provision trade and occasional part-time work provided the natives with benefits beyond those available directly through trade. Of course, the system also ensured a profitable trade for the fur companies.

The HBC's monopoly of the Mackenzie River trade provided a substantial brake on the natives' attempts to secure even greater returns. Their usefulness as trappers, provisioners, interpreters, and casual labourers prevented the firm from treating them too harshly, but the absence of competitive traders limited the Indians' ability to extract economic concessions. Indians in the Yukon River valley found it much easier to challenge the HBC, primarily because they possessed trading alternatives. The natives encouraged rivalries, and informed post officers of the activities of competing traders. When necessary, they concocted stories about the Russians or coastal traders in an effort to secure better prices. The natives trading at Fort Youcon told the post traders almost every year that the Russians were but a short distance downstream and that a military attack was imminent.

There were other strategies available. The natives readily recognized the fur traders' vulnerability. With only a dozen or so traders encamped in the midst of several thousand natives, and with the white men's fears only too evident on occasion, the natives could capitalize on the force of their numbers. The Indians around Fort Youcon several times threatened the traders with violence if their demands were not met. The threats assumed special menace after the Tlingit destroyed Campbell's post, Fort Selkirk, in 1852. Such bellicose behaviour was unusual.

A more regular, and more effective, means of exacting concessions was the witholding of furs. Efforts to get the HBC to reduce prices for trade goods failed, largely because of the unsettling impact such a measure would have had on the Mackenzie trade. Still, this bargaining tool did force the firm to adapt their trading practices to suit native demands and even to replace employees the Indians disliked. By capitalizing on, or inventing, competition, and by threatening physical or economic retaliation, the natives were able to force major alterations in the northern fur trade.

Disruptions of the Native Way of Life

This first intrusion of Europeans into the north proved, in many ways, far less disruptive than those that followed. The fur trade drew on native strengths and skills, and created a mutually dependent economic system. Although the Dene could and did ignore the trade for a time, their increasing reliance on European goods had tied them to the trading posts. Subsistence hunting expanded to include provisioning the men of the forts and the fur brigades. This combination accelerated demands on local resources, just as involvement in the company's trading system diverted the natives, in part at least, from their normal seasonal rounds.

Historian A.J. Ray offers a provocative analysis of this process. Most commentators see the establishment of post-World War II social programmes as the turning point in native dependence on Canadian assistance, but Ray suggests that reliance can be traced to the nineteenth-century fur trade. He argues that the use of credit, the encouragement of economic specialization, and the depletion of resources created a welfare environment designed to serve the HBC's interests. As Ray concluded:

> In many areas of the north, it was in the company's interest and ability to perpetuate the use of a credit/ barter or truck system until the late nineteenth century. The arrangement discouraged, and often prevented, Indians from leaving this part of the primary resource sector of the economy, even in regions where resources were so depleted that only marginal livelihoods could be sustained....In summary, the HBC was partly responsible for limiting the ability of Indians to adjust to the new economic circumstances at the beginning of this century. Debt-ridden, repeatedly blocked from alternative opportunities for over a century, and accustomed to various forms of relief over two centuries, Indians became so evidently demoralized in this century, but the groundwork for this was laid in the more distant past.

Even given the importance of the economic reorganization, the erosion of skills struck more directly at the core of native life. The introduction of firearms, although they were initially not as reliable or accurate as often supposed, gradually supplanted spears and bows and arrows. The availability of metal tools at the trading post meant that the shaped bone implements could be discarded, and the age-old skill of making those tools disappeared. Toward the end of the nineteenth century, natives began to purchase more southern clothing. That also represented a challenge to traditional craft work. The old skills disappeared slowly, maintained by the older people, but often shunned by a younger generation raised in the shadow of the trading post. Few people, native or white, mourned or even noticed the loss, although in times of hardship and following the contraction of the trading frontier those skills would be dearly missed.

Even more profound was the effect of disease. The HBC trading routes, which spanned the prairies, descended the Mackenzie and crossed the Rocky and Richardson Mountains, became a conduit for European illnesses. To the west, native trade routes similarly provided a ready passage for diseases originating far outside the region. Trading patterns also exacerbated the spread of disease. Indians gathered annually at the posts, where they came in contact with sick traders. Then the natives dispersed throughout the region as befit their role as middlemen, unknowingly carrying diseases along with the trade goods.

The Indians had no natural immunity to these "virgin soil epidemics," and diseases that passed with little serious impact among European populations killed thousands of native people. Without natural protection, unfamiliar with the symptoms, and unsure of the appropriate treatment, the natives responded to the diseases with fear and panic.

A scarlet fever epidemic in 1865 provides a particularly graphic example of the process by which the disease spread. Members of the annual supply boat crew carrying an outfit from Fort Simpson to Fort Youcon contracted scarlet fever. Although often so weakened by disease that they could scarcely pilot their craft, they pushed on, determined to deliver the supplies and thus prevent hardship among company employees at the northern posts. They passed the highly contagious fever to the vulnerable natives along their route. The disease spread with stunning power and severity, leaving hundreds dead in its wake. At Fort Youcon alone, between 170 and 200 local natives succumbed.

A variety of European diseases, including measles, mumps and influenza were brought north in those early years. The natives struggled to interpret the intimidating devastation in the framework of their own spiritual beliefs, and initially attributed the illnesses to European sorcery. As one trader commented, ''No Indian dies a natural death, but is killed by the conjurations of another at some distance, and this superstition is the cause of much blood shed among them.'' The traditional appeal to the spirits and to the power of the shamans proved to be little defense against these unfamiliar and fearsome diseases.

With sparse statistical data and literary evidence restricted to observations of the effect on natives living near the posts, it is difficult to assess the cumulative impact of the diseases. It is also likely that pre-contact trading networks introduced the alien illnesses many years before Europeans actually entered the area. Anthropologist Shepherd Krech III has argued that the Kutchin had a population of about 5400 people in the early nineteenth century. By the 1860s, numerous diseases reduced that number to around 900. If that ratio is assumed to be roughly constant for the entire north — and evidence from the upper Mackenzie and the Yukon valley supports Krech's analysis — the demographic impact of European expansion was, in the north as elsewhere across North America, truly devastating.

Changes in the social and religious order further unsettled a native society already facing a new economic order and reeling from disease. The northern traders were overwhelmingly single, unattached men. As elsewhere, company traders in the north sought comfort and sexual solace from native women. The natives accepted the liaisons for a variety of reasons. Life in the trading post often meant a higher standard of living, better food and less work than in a native camp. The women also played an important economic role for their band. By serving as interpreters and go-betweens, they assisted with the fur trade.

The timing of northward expansion prevented social contact from mirroring completely conditions in the south. The development of the Red River settlement, the arrival of Anglican missionaries, and Governor George Simpson's decision to abandon his native partner in favour of a white wife combined to eliminate social approval for permanent relationships with Indian and even mixed blood women. When the HBC joined in the chorus of Victorian moralizing, the upper ranks of the firm's servants listened. Those desiring corporate mobility were well advised not to marry native women. Robert Campbell wrote that Governor Simpson had told him "Now, Campbell, don't you get married as we want you for active service."

The new social order was highlighted when Alexander Hunter Murray's new white wife accompanied him north in 1847. Though the weight of corporate disapproval had its impact, it did not stop the inevitable social and sexual contact with the natives. Officers shied away from permanent arrangements, though less formal liaisons continued, usually on the quiet. Among the lower ranks, more regular marriages were common. American explorer William Dall suggested the company

actually encouraged such relationships: "Every effort
is made, to make these men [company servants] marry
Indian wives; thus forcing them to remain in the country by burdening them with females whom they are
ashamed to take back to civilization and cannot desert."
The relationships further disrupted native society. The
removal of native women reduced the number of
females remaining in the Indian bands, thus making it
more difficult for young native men to find partners.
Dall's comment notwithstanding, white men often left
the north when their contracts expired. Some took their
wives and families south, others abandoned them. The
fur traders were therefore more than just men of
commerce. They represented yet another element of
uncertainty in the quickly changing social conditions
of northern fur trade society.

The Missionaries

As if these forces were not enough, the opening of the
region by the traders ensured a rapid expansion of
missionary activities among the Dene. Given the zeal
of both the Protestant and Roman Catholic missionaries in the nineteenth century, it is hardly surprising
that the north would emerge as a major mission field.
The north contained the prime elements for evangel-
ism: a primitive, pagan people in need of Christian
salvation, little degradation of the "child-like" natives
by Europeans, and scant prospect for immediate settlement. The missionaries rushed north, anxious to save,
convert, and "civilize" the Indians before the inevitable destructive effects of white expansion were visited
upon them. The clerics approached their task with a
combination of Christian hope and fear that the task
might be too great. As Church Missionary Society

worker William Bompas noted, "These mountain Loucheux [Kutchin] seem 'the lowest of all people.' But I cannot help hoping that they are a "chosen race.''

The late timing of the HBC's expansion allowed both the Church Missionary Society (Anglican) and its bitter rival, the Roman Catholic Oblates of Mary Immaculate to approach the north simultaneously. The company had typically been of two minds as to the utility of missionary endeavours, welcoming the attempt to civilize the natives, but concerned that the missionary preoccupation with settlement and non-traditional pursuits would interfere with harvesting. In a move symbolic of the forthcoming battle for native souls, both Anglican archdeacon James Hunter and Oblate priest Henry Grollier came to Fort Simpson in 1858.

Competition for native souls proved vigorous and even bitter. The Church Missionary Society received invaluable aid from the HBC, which clearly favoured the Anglican missions. Company men went so far as to threaten to cut off trade with natives who visited the Catholic priests. Although a concern for public relations prevented an overt assault on the Catholics, the firm's men ostracized many of the early priests and offered only what assistance was absolutely necessary. This ironically served to bring the Catholics closer to their native communicants. While Anglican missionaries often lived with the fur traders, Catholic priests were forced to live outside the post and sup with the natives and mixed bloods. The Catholics quickly became entrenched among the natives along the Mackenzie River, but the joint effort of the Church Missionary Society and the HBC kept the Oblates out of the Yukon.

The Catholics seemed better suited for northern mission work. With exemplary zeal — plus a vow to a life of poverty, which reduced costs — the priests commited themselves to a charge for which they had received specific training. They often stayed with one community for their entire career, learning the local language, travelling with their congregations, and adapting to the rigours of northern life. A few Anglican clergy, like the venerable Bishop Bompas and particularly Robert McDonald (an early Yukon missionary and long-time resident at Fort McPherson), operated much like the Catholics. Most, however, viewed their native work as a transitional phase in their careers. Often without missionary training, carrying middle-class ambitions, and seldom adequately prepared for northern life, Anglican missionaries rarely stayed in the region for long. Bompas appealed to the Church Missionary Society to take care in sending men and women to the north. He asked for only "those of an inferior grade [who] in going to the far west generally rise a peg which is mostly pleasant to themselves and their neighbours."

Language was the most obvious barrier to understanding. Although the Catholic priests worked hard to learn native dialects, and such Anglicans as McDonald, Bompas and Canham did the same among their charges, it proved a difficult undertaking. The Anglican tradition of moving clergy about regularly often undermined months of serious language study.

Although the two religious groups shared a common goal, there was virtually no cooperation. Both believed their spiritual interpretations and religious path offered salvation and, equally, that the opposing faith offered only false hope. The Anglicans commited themselves to fending off the "Papist" and "Romanist" challenge. Catholic missionaries complained that the Anglicans were spreading rumours about the priests' sexual habits, but they were no kinder in their attacks on the Church Missionary Society workers. Both groups hastened to mark out their territory, struggling to baptize and hence lay claim to as many natives as they could before their rivals arrived. The "rush for souls" hardly endeared the missionaries to the natives, nor did it provide a useful model of Christian ethics at work. The endless back-stabbing and name-calling substantially hampered the missionaries' efforts.

The cumulative impact of the missionaries' work is difficult to assess. The stakes were high. Christian teachings, particularly the concept of a single deity and codified spiritual beliefs, struck at the heart of the loosely formed, individualistic, and animist beliefs held by the Indians. The increasing number of baptisms, marriages and funerals, and the appearance of lay readers and ordained Indian clergy, lent credence to missionary claims that they had indeed wrought a spiritual revolution in the north. There were, however, real limits to conversion, and missionary "body counts" must be treated with considerable scepticism.

While natives often adopted the forms of faith, such outward manifestations did not necessarily signal total conversion. The natives' spirituality was their world view, a way of explaining a wide range of natural phenomena. The Christian message, as broad as it was, did not aspire to replace the full range of native beliefs. It was therefore both possible and even logical that the contrasting spiritual systems would amalgamate. In several areas, particularly among the Kutchin, shamans became lay readers, thus retaining much of their spiritual authority. The natives' response in times of distress illustrated the persistence of pre-Christian beliefs. When starvation, disease or other hardship threatened, Indians regularly turned to traditional rituals in search of help, either instead of, or in addition to, their appeals to the missionaries.

The Oblates won the battle for converts in much of the Mackenzie River valley, largely because of their greater flexibility and sensitivity to native culture. The Anglicans were not without their victories, for they could claim almost the entire Yukon and northern Mackenzie as their exclusive preserves. Commentators have long assumed that the natives succumbed to the missionaries' preaching because of the weakness of their own society. John Webster Grant concluded that "Conversion to Christianity was essentially a phenomenon of the moon of wintertime, when ancestral spirits had ceased to perform their expected functions." While this analysis may apply elsewhere, it seems not to apply to the Dene, who faced the Christain challenge while their social and economic order remained strong and they remained confident of their future. As Kerry Abel has recently demonstrated:

> The Dene were not easily, automatically and happily "converted" to Christianity or to other values which the European missionaries attempted to teach. Some rejected the message entirely and openly, some listened cautiously and politely so as not to offend, still others adopted elements of Christian teaching which seemed appropriate to individual cases. There was no single response in this individualistic society. As a pragmatic people, they tested the new ideas and accepted only those which proved their utility.

Most Indians became social Christians, adopting the services, hymns and ceremonies of the new faith. Their spiritual absorption came much more slowly.

The missionaries' major impact was felt on the social rather than spiritual front. The clerics found much they opposed in native society, including polygamy, infanticide, the potlatch and the treatment of women and the aged. The natives seemed to give up some practices readily, recognizing that the white men's disapproval could interfere with trade and general relations. It would be inaccurate to suggest that the natives simply succumbed to the missionaries' entreaties, for they had demonstrated their ability to resist such pressures many times in the past. The Anglican and Catholic clergy continued to work on their biblical translations, studied native languages, and sought the acceptance of their Indian communicants. As they did so, they worked very hard to alter social behaviour deemed "pagan" and "unchristian," not without some success.

Signs of Change

In little over half a century, the north had been transformed. The expansion of the European commercial empire forced numerous economic adjustments, ones the natives made, for the most part, willingly. The arrival of the Europeans simultaneously introduced disease and the disruption of native society through inter-marriage. The missionaries added to the upheaval. The restructuring of the north had just begun, however, and as the end of the nineteenth century approached, the intensity of white activity increased and the fur trade lost its dominant position.

The changes appeared first in the Yukon River valley. The American purchase of Alaska from Russia in 1867 opened the lower Yukon River to development. "Yankee" traders, aided by a sympathetic government, pushed upstream and by 1869 the HBC had been ordered to quit Fort Youcon. The company pulled back toward what became, in 1870, Canadian soil, but the loss of the strategic position had destroyed the HBC's dominance in the regional trade. The company's returns dwindled rapidly, and even the post Indians who had initially followed the company eastward abandoned it to trade with the Americans. The field now lay open for American firms and, ignoring the same border they had demanded the HBC observe, they extended their trade well inside Canadian territory. The Alaska Commercial Company soon supplanted the HBC in the Yukon valley fur trade.

The British company's monopoly lay broken, as free trade in the south and the American challenge in the far northwest chipped away at the firm's once mighty empire. The sale of Rupert's Land to Canada and the beginnings of settlement on the prairies convinced the firm to shift its priorities southward. Its northern fur trade continued, but was no longer the company's sole reason for existence. In the Yukon River valley, the entire fur trade soon dropped to second place. The expansion of the mining frontier replaced the exchange of animal skins as the region's economic cornerstone. The fur trade society developed in the Yukon during the HBC period faded into the background.

Sealed off from the Yukon, the Mackenzie River valley was the last bastion of the company's once vaunted monopoly. The legal right to control the trade had disappeared, but aggressive trading measures allowed the firm to maintain a practical monopoly. But improvements to transportation along the southern Mackenzie during the Klondike gold rush finally broke the commercial blockade. Opposition traders could now challenge the HBC directly.

The fur trade had drawn Europeans north, and the distinctive society that followed the trade across the continents moved into the region as well. Before the grand upheaval of the Klondike gold rush began, the fur trade had already recast native occupation of the north. Although subsequent developments would again alter the economic and social fabric, the basic elements of native-white relations established during the fur trade period would remain a permanent feature of life in the north. As a new order pushed the HBC from the Yukon, the north had found a new place in the southern imagination.

3
The Gold Frontier and the Klondike

The most famous photo in northern Canadian history shows a long, thin line of men filing up a steep cliff. The site was the Chilkoot Pass, a small notch in the coastal mountains long used by the Tlingit Indians to reach the headwaters of the Yukon River. The year was 1897. These were not Indians, however, and their purpose for hauling the heavy packs up the hillside was not to trade with the interior natives. The men in the photo were "cheechakos" — newcomers heading for the newly discovered goldfields of the Klondike.

The brief, intense sensation of the Klondike gold rush has dominated southern images of the north since the initial discovery in 1896. The migration of tens of thousands of would-be prospectors into the sparsely inhabited Yukon River valley rapidly uprooted existing economic and social relations, and provided a severe test of Canada's commitment to its northern territories. The story does not begin in 1896, but rather with the gradual unfolding of the North American mining frontier.

The search for gold was an ever-present theme around the world in the nineteenth century. In an era of economic growth, when capitalism and industrialization reigned supreme, the age-old fascination with this unique metal assumed new urgency. Along the frontiers of North America, Africa, and Australia, prospectors reached beyond the borders of agricultural settlement in search of the proverbial "Mother Lode." Their travels carried risks, as they were often unprepared for the challenging environment they faced. Even more, their Euro-centric chauvinism taught them to disdain the native populations, which were quickly shunted aside if paying ore was discovered. The desire for a major strike fed on the "get rich quick" mentality of the age, and the public followed developments on the frontier with rapt attention. The prospectors were also tracked by claim jumpers, prostitutes, and card sharks — the ones who mined the miners — together creating a boisterous, often violent society on the fringes of social control.

North American gold rush towns were, by their dependence on a concentrated non-renewable resource, quintessential "boom-and-bust" societies. The decline of the gold deposit followed the discovery, leaving a ghost town as the sole reminder of the brief days of glory. Though the goldfields were soon exhausted, other developments usually came after, building on the infrastructure erected during the previous mining phase, and more permanent communities emerged. The Yukon was the site of the last great gold rush, and passed through all the stages from discovery to rush to exhaustion of the resource. But the last stage did not follow; the Klondike gold rush did not initiate further development and settlement for the Yukon.

The prospectors came to the Yukon River valley on the last stage of a moving frontier that had crossed the entire continent. Miners had slowly pushed westward across the United States through the early nineteenth century. The mining frontier crept westward until prospectors uncovered a major goldfield in California in 1847. By the 1850s, prospectors reached British

territory and were scouring the shores of the lower
Fraser River. A new discovery of gold touched off
another rush.

In less than three decades, the mining frontier had
expanded from California to the farthest reaches of
British Columbia. It left in its wake abandoned mines,
hills denuded of trees, and creek beds diverted and
reshaped by the miners. The gold rushes had also
ushered in a new era for the mining districts. In British
Columbia, the authority of the formerly powerful HBC
waned in the face of the miners' onslaught, leaving
the field open to farmers, ranchers and other settlers.
The legacy of the gold rush was therefore two-sided.
It altered previous economic and social systems which,
in British Columbia as in the north, had placed the
natives in a strong position vis-à-vis the European traders. The miners served as a disruptive first wave for
the settlement frontier, displacing the natives and
bringing in their wake a transportation, service, and
government infrastructure which would form the basis
for a new, white British Columbia.

This mining frontier, which at its height could be
boisterous and aggressive, reached quietly into the
Yukon River valley. Arthur Harper and Leroy ''Jack''
McQuesten led a small party of miners into the region
in 1873, but they enjoyed little success. A few other
prospectors followed, scratching at the banks of the
Yukon and Stewart Rivers. Even when George Holt
became the first white man to cross from the Pacific
coast to the upper Yukon River valley few miners were
prepared to risk the dangers and isolation of the far
north as long as returns remained unproven.

A modest regional society emerged around the Forty-
mile mining district, where some 250 miners had gathered by the mid-1880s. The returns, perhaps $15 a

day from one of the better claims, may have touched off a minor rush elsewhere. The high cost of supplies and the great distances involved removed much of the lustre from these early developments. The miners continued their search for the big strike, forming loose partnerships as they scoured the various creeks. The limited scale of the Yukon goldfields did not prevent the emergence of a unique placer-mining society and economy.

The social order was very individualistic. There was a certain community spirit, a commitment that news of a strike be quickly shared, and that resources necessary for survival not be withheld from those in need. But the philosophical root of the mining society was individual initiative and personal reward. The placer-mining technology imposed its own constraints. Methods for sifting through the gold-bearing gravel remained labour intensive. At first, the miners sifted through the loose gravel on exposed sand bars, unable to penetrate the permafrost below. Then William Ogilvie of the Geological Survey of Canada convinced the miners to build fires on the frozen ground, removing the loosened dirt as the heat penetrated the permafrost. This allowed the miners to continue throughout the winter, although the work in a shaft driven down to bedrock was hardly pleasant. The system of stockpiling dirt until spring, then running it through a sluice-box designed to catch the gold dust and nuggets was rather primitive, but it served its purpose. Most miners worked alone or with a single partner. Only a few miners with "proved" claims could afford to hire additional help.

The Yukon mining district slowly took shape, although the diggings on the Stewart River soon played out. Forty-mile, a rustic shantytown with few amenities in the early years, gradually assumed a settled air. A major discovery continued to elude the miners but most of those with claims earned a respectable income. The Alaska Commercial Company tapped that modest wealth by running a regular steamship service along the Yukon River. The rough-hewn frontier town was slowly being tamed. A few women arrived to join their husbands, William Bompas opened an Anglican mission, and more stores and taverns opened to serve the miners. The fact that the creeks were barely inside Canadian territory was of little consequence, for the majority of the miners were Americans. In the absence of demonstrated Canadian sovereignty, the community developed along American lines.

The early mining district hardly seemed headed for a boom. Although the modest returns seemed assured, the region held little appeal for the non-professional miner. Some miners left every year, worn out by the fruitless toil of a barren claim, but a few more came in, searching for the discovery that would trigger a new gold rush. Some of the new arrivals hired out as labourers, trying to raise money for their own "grub-stake." Those looking for a more regular income hired on as clerks with the trading companies. The two main commercial firms, the Alaska Commercial Company and the Northern Commercial Company, diversified their interests. They served the miners, but maintained an active role in the still-profitable fur trade.

For natives living close to the miners, the pre-Klon-dike developments offered both enticements and dangers. The miners, as was their wont, brought liquor, a commodity previously unavailable from Russian or HBC traders. The natives soon found pleasure in the "hi-you" time associated with alcohol, including the famous "hootch" that they soon learned to brew themselves. The inter-racial drinking parties were less frequent and less damaging than local missionaries repeatedly alleged, but the spectre of drunken Indians was always sure to get government attention. Most miners came north alone, and the isolation of the Forty-mile camp precluded a regular migration of white women. So, as the fur traders had done, miners regularly sought female companionship in the native camps. They preferred short-term liaisons, typically in conjunction with drinking parties. The Reverend R.J. Bowen commented, "The white prospectors had been thoughtless enough to lure the Indian squaws into their home(s) and into the dance hall. The results of such action was seen in the number of half-breed children." The missionaries castigated the miners for their behaviour; their fury mounted when reports surfaced of miners buying native wives (usually young girls). Some men married the women in the country fashion, joining with their wives' families and living in the "Indian way." While tolerant of short-term liaisons, the white community strongly disapproved of those "squaw-men" who willingly "lowered" themselves to live with the natives.

Most natives only sampled the new economic and social order. They joined the drinking parties while in camp, but their visits were infrequent and the consumption of alcohol did not breed the violence and debauchery the missionaries feared. The continued attractiveness of harvesting furs kept the Indians away from the camps, except to trade furs, sell meat, purchase supplies, and occasionally seek work. Strong racial discrimination in the camps ensured that there were few jobs for those few natives who sought entry.

Yet the mining economy still provided opportunities for the Indians. The miners needed food, so suppliers of moose and caribou meat, and fish for dog teams found a ready market. Although the miners and trading companies preferred white labourers, the supply was so limited that they were often forced to turn to native helpers to unload steamers or transport supplies from the Yukon River to the mine sites. Native workers consistently received lower wages than their white counterparts — the white men insisted upon it — but the income satisfied most of the Indians' needs at the trading post, for the fur trade continued much as before. The economic changes of the early mining frontier had, as during the fur trade period, worked substantially to the natives' benefit.

The missionaries, particularly the venerable Bishop Bompas, refused to see the Indians' situation this way. Bompas constantly appealed to the Canadian government for help, hoping to protect his native charges from the perceived and anticipated depredations of the white population. Bompas also asked the Canadian government to assert its sovereignty over the area before the American occupation assumed political legitimization. His most telling argument, though, lay not with the natives' condition or questions of territorial control, but with the revelation that miners and traders leaving the area regularly took thousands of dollars in gold and furs without paying excise duties. Bompas' complaints were echoed by several businessmen who saw government intervention as an opportunity to compete more equitably with American companies which violated the border with impunity. The Canadian government heard the arguments but they saw little need for a show of force in the far north. When faced with a similar threat on the southern plains, the government had created the North West Mounted Police (NWMP) and despatched them westward. But the prairies were deemed central to the country's survival. The government and people of Canada could see no such role for the distant and frozen northland.

Federal representatives had been north before Bompas first raised his complaints. Those men belonged with the Geological Survey of Canada, a branch of government dedicated to the surveying and scientific exploration of the country. William Ogilvie, George Dawson and Robert McConnell had surveyed the Yukon and Mackenzie River basins, and the Tyrell brothers, James and Joseph, had examined the Keewatin District. The modest mining ventures in the region, however, had developed independently of survey activities and subsequent discoveries occurred with little help from government geologists. The advance of the GSC did not, therefore, signal imminent southern interest in the north.

The NWMP symbolized the extension of Canadian sovereignty in western and northern Canada. When the advances of American whiskey traders threatened the plans of John A. Macdonald's Conservative government for the peaceful agricultural settlement of the plains, the NWMP had been created. Although the force had been established as a temporary expedient, it quickly demonstrated its usefulness as an instrument of Canadian sovereignty. It was only logical when the government decided it needed a greater formal presence in the Yukon River valley that it turned to the NWMP. However, the reaction was far from swift. Only when Bompas' complaints were reinforced by complaints from businessmen about unregulated trade did the matter assume any urgency. The dominance of ''Yankee'' prospectors on Canadian soil touched a deep-seated fear of American expansionism and finally forced the government to act.

The NWMP, responding to government orders, dispatched a two-man expedition to the Yukon. Inspector Charles Constantine and Staff Sergeant Charles Brown entered via the Chilkoot Pass and travelled along the Yukon River to the Forty-mile camp. Constantine did not find the raucous mining camp that he had been led to expect. The small community was quiet and surprisingly professional. Reports of excessive drinking and gambling, he claimed, were exaggerated, although a negative view of the natives clouded his opinion of community relations. Constantine carried a special commission from the Department of Indian Affairs. The department's policy for the northern Indians was spelled out clearly in his instructions ''not to give encouragement to the idea that they (the natives) will be received into treaty, and taken under the care of the government.'' The federal government reserved treaties for areas of impending permanent development, and the limited mining potential of the Yukon River valley simply did not point in that direction.

Constantine recommended that a force of thirty-five to forty constables be sent north. His report was well received in official circles, although the actual complement was scaled down considerably. The Canadian government was prepared to assert its sovereignty in the north — in particular to protect the integrity of the border and to enforce Canadian laws. But few officials were prepared to take the next step of incorporating the north into the grandiose development and settlement schemes then in place for the west. It was, however, a start. Canada was officially going north and the largely American mining population would finally have to recognize the significance of residing on Canadian soil.

The return of Constantine with a contingent of twenty men, and the establishment of Fort Cudahy in the summer of 1895 carried great symbolic importance. The force did more than carry the Union Jack northward; it brought as well the full range of Canadian laws and the means of enforcing them. The extensions posed a potential clash between the Canadian and American frontiers. The individualistic, democratic "Yankees" had established their own form of local justice. Rough laws — those necessary for community survival under such conditions — were developed and enforced through semi-formal miners' meetings. These gatherings, which found their inspiration in the long tradition of American vigilante justice, provided a widely accepted forum for settling debts and disputes over claims, and even for handling criminal cases. A meeting could be called by any miner seeking redress, or by the community at large when an offender had been caught. The decision of the assembled group was binding, and penalties, including fines or banishment from the mines, were imposed. The meetings did not follow legal procedures and conventions. This exercise in direct democracy was subject to domination by cliques, favouritism and rash decisions, but did ultimately provide a workable system of rough justice in an otherwise lawless environment.

When the NWMP arrived, Canadian justice collided with the American frontier tradition. It was no contest. In the spring of 1896, the miners at Glacier Creek met and seized a claim in an attempt to force the owners to pay back wages. The owners appealed to the police. Constantine recognized "that this was the turning point, and should I give them their way or recognize them in any manner, trouble would never cease." He ignored the decision of the miners' meeting and ensured that the owners remained in possession of their claim. As historian W.R. Morrison argued, "American-style frontier democracy had been replaced by British authoritarian paternalism." The transition proved surprisingly smooth, partly because of the greater military force contained within the NWMP detachment, but more because the miners placed far greater importance on the maintenance of order than on preserving their modest experiment in self-government. The arrival of the NWMP steered the Yukon mining fields away from their American frontier course and ensured that Canadian laws, customs duties, mining regulations, and legislative initiatives would carry the day. Even before the gold rush, the Canadian legal model had replaced the American.

The course of northern history took a dramatic turn in the summer of 1896. George Carmack, written off by most local miners as an unreliable "squaw man," followed the advice of prospector Robert Henderson and did some work on the tributaries of the Klondike River along with two native companions, Skookum Jim and Tagish Charlie. On August 17, 1896, at Rabbit (later renamed Bonanza) Creek, Skookum Jim made the first discovery of the gold-lined creek beds that touched off the Klondike gold rush. Carmack moved swiftly to broadcast news of the strike.

Forty-mile became a ghost town overnight, as almost every miner in the district rushed to claim their share of the new Eldorado. By the summer of 1897, before news of the strike reached the "outside," the creeks surrounding the Bonanza had been staked, and a community of some 4,000 men had sprung up at the confluence of the Klondike and Yukon Rivers. Merchants moved to the new town of Dawson almost as quickly as the miners. Prospectors arriving at the creeks as early as January 1897 found most of the gold-bearing ground staked. Latecomers fought over fractions of land between improperly filed claims, or sought new discoveries on nearby creeks. The choice claims and the greatest opportunities had been taken even before word of the northern Bonanza reached the south.

The legendary swarm of would-be prospectors who assaulted the mountain passes to reach Dawson did not even begin for at least a year after the initial discovery. In the spring of 1897, the miners washed their winter's diggings and confirmed the magnitude of the first strike. A number of prospectors, flushed with their success, left for the south. When their ships docked in San Francisco and Seattle, news of the dramatic discovery swept across North America like a prairie fire. The American newspapers, practitioners of the art of "yellow journalism," fanned the flames. Through creative and, when necessary, inventive reporting, the papers developed news events into media sensations. The Klondike story contained all the right elements: exotic location, great wealth, high adventure, and danger. Headlines screaming of fabulous wealth and untold opportunities were a powerful tonic for the unemployed or disenchanted. Publishing houses rushed into print guidebooks purporting to explain laws, conditions, and material needs for prospecting in the north.

The rush itself contained all the elements of a tragicomedy. Promoters touted a stupefying array of transportation devices deemed capable of crossing the northern tundra, and offered dazzling new techniques for extracting gold from the permafrost; it was a huckster's paradise. The wave gathered strength as it crossed North America. Cheechakos gathered in Vancouver,

Seattle and San Francisco. If they escaped from the gamblers, thieves and con artists, they could find passage north to Dyea or Skagway, the gateways to the Yukon. These two American port towns, located at the bottom of the Chilkoot and White Passes, attracted thousands of ill-equipped adventurers. Many fell by the wayside here. Out of money or disenchanted, they turned back. There were other routes to the Klondike. Those with money paid for passage on sternwheelers plying the Yukon River. Others succumbed to the faulty advertising of the small town of Edmonton, and sought to reach Dawson City by way of one of the trails heading north from the prairie city.

And the miners kept coming, even as information on the over-crowded goldfields, harsh climate, and poor prospects filtered south. A few prospectors reached the Yukon in 1897, but most planned to arrive the following year. They crossed the mountain passes in the winter of 1897 and waited in a tent city of some 10,000 at Lake Lindeman for the ice to move in the spring. The toil of carrying supplies from the coast to the headwaters of the Yukon exacted its toll, and offered an early test of the prospectors' commitment to the Klondike mirage. Some gave up and exchanged their grubstake for return fare. Most pressed on. In 1898 alone, more than 30,000 people headed for Dawson City.

The migration was not unguarded, for the NWMP closely observed every part of the passage across Canadian territory. Inspector Constantine requested more men as soon as the magnitude of the Rabbit Creek discovery became known. The government responded slowly, but Constantine had ninety-five men by the fall of 1897 and almost 200 by the following spring. The men were needed, for the vast majority of the "stampeders" were Americans, and Canadian control of its far northwest seemed again under attack. This was a battle that the police were determined to win before it began. Prospectors crossing to Canadian territory from Dyea or Skagway found a NWMP outpost at the height of the pass. The police exacted customs duties, turned back any deemed "undesirable" (though this practice was against the law) and, most importantly, ensured that each person entering the territory carried a year's supply of food (1,150 pounds). This latter requirement weeded out the ill-prepared and prevented starvation in the goldfields.

The NWMP also wanted to prevent the licentiousness of Skagway from spreading inland. There were murders, thefts and other crimes along the gold rush trail, but the NWMP controlled the "evil" element, quickly and effectively "got their man," and halted the spread of American-style frontier development and its close partner, vigilante justice.

The police were only one obstacle on the gold trail. The prospectors, gathered on the shores at Lake Lindeman or Lake Bennett, needed a craft to carry themselves and their supplies to Dawson. The surrounding hills were soon denuded of trees as every scrap of available timber was used for boat construction. When the ice moved in the spring, a flotilla of several thousand unlikely rafts and boats followed. Travellers in the early spring faced bitter cold, rain and snow as they set out on the final leg of their journey. The course across several large lakes and along the Yukon River was generally uneventful, although the dangerous waters of Miles Canyon and White Horse Rapids stood in the way. The Yukon River carved a more leisurely course northward, broken by the less threatening Five Finger and Rink Rapids, and the prospectors poled their vessels through the rapidly lengthening days of early summer.

Those who reached Dawson carried a well-earned sense of accomplishment, for many had been left in their wake. But that temporary euphoria soon gave way to disappointment. The streets were not paved with gold, but rather with prodigious amounts of mud, and the shanties, tents and hastily constructed buildings offered a far from impressive visage. Thousands of men and a handful of women crammed the streets, bars, hotels, and brothels. Gold was in evidence everywhere; gold dust and nuggets were the standard currency in the region. But the star-struck stampeders soon discovered that all the good land had been staked. Some refused to be deterred and headed for the creeks. The credulous "prospectors" proved an easy mark for those with a worked out or worthless claim. A few of the latecomers did strike it rich, often by ignoring the established "rules" of prospecting and trying their luck in such improbable places as the sides of hills that had formerly been creek beds. For the majority, however, the arrival in Dawson was the only triumph. Realising their folly, and often embarrassed at their naïveté, many sold their outfits at the current grossly inflated prices and bought passage for the "outside."

Dawson City

Dawson City was, in one historian's phrase, "an unsophisticated mining camp built on a bog." Despite its impermanent and ramshackle appearance, Dawson was, in fact, a city, for a NWMP census of 1898 indicated a population of 16,000 (omitting those on the creeks). But Dawson hardly rated the comparison sometimes made to San Francisco. A few prominent buildings along the main street added substance to the city's profile, but Dawson remained an unattractive mining camp, similar in every way but size to earlier communities at Forty-mile and Circle City.

In the populace of the frontier boom-town, Americans predominated, ensuring that United States national holidays took precedence over Canadian celebrations. The miners, some of them extremely wealthy, were excellent customers for the saloon-keepers, gamblers, and prostitutes who followed the prospectors north. Although a few stalwart citizens protested the practices of these "langorous lillies of soulless love," they were tolerated by civic authorities and the police. Even so, the image of a bawdy, lawless town, promoted by the journalists because it sold newspapers, hardly matched reality, for such social evils never dominated the young town.

The NWMP played a crucial role in regulating the spread of vice, though they took a more pragmatic approach than Klondike mythology suggests. Comptroller Fred White hinted at the police's approach when he rather caustically noted, "It is difficult to convince the goody-goody people that in the development and settlement of a new country allowances must be made for the excesses of human behaviour." The police could be strict, as they were on the questions of handguns and working on Sunday, but were also prepared to be flexible. They accepted gambling and prostitution as unstoppable and instead tried to ensure that the customers received fair exchange for their money. Stroller White, an American journalist, commented that Dawson was

> far from being a model for the Young People's Society of Christian Endeavour but there was a gaiety and

lightheartedness about its sinning that was absent in Skagway. And while Dawson provided plenty of places and opportunities for suckers to dispose of their money, the suckers were never steered, dragooned and bootjacketed into these places as they had been in Skagway.

The police themselves were not immune to sins of the flesh, and many were discharged or sentenced to a term in the gaol for cavorting with prostitutes, being drunk in public, or otherwise breaking the force's moral code. It is small wonder that there were not more difficulties with the police. As W.R. Morrison, historian of the police, wrote:

> The police were exceedingly ill-paid; during the Klondike period the basic rate of pay for a constable was fifty cents a day.... In addition, men on Yukon service were given fifty cents a day hardship allowance. In contrast, common labourers in Dawson could make between five and ten dollars a day in wages....

The NWMP were also more than law enforcement officers. In fact, the bulk of their work consisted of the rather mundane tasks of local government. The police carried the mail, served as health inspectors, and registered claims. By dumping these duties on the poorly paid police, the federal government was able to cut costs, centralize administration, and postpone permanent civil service appointments.

Because they were so active in so many fields, the Mounties became a key element in the popular perception of the Klondike, as represented by the turn-of-the-century pulp literature. Southerners trying to comprehend this northern adventure had trouble escaping the myths. The immortalization of the Klondike quest in the poetry of Robert Service, the novels of Jack London, and the historical reconstructions of Pierre Berton emphasize the heroic, the unique and the cold. The reality, though, was less romantic.

Natives and the Gold Rush

Although the images of the north focus on Dawson City, the gold rush affected a much broader area. Natives throughout the region felt the brunt of this overwhelmingly white event. The racial accommodation established in the pre-gold rush mining frontier evaporated in the rush to the Klondike.

A reading of the massive literature on the gold rush reveals the limited native role in the event. With few exceptions, Indians shied away from the dubious pleasures of Dawson City. Anglican missionaries and the police encouraged this isolation. To Bishop Bompas, the effort to segregate the natives — even if it required extra-legal measures on occasion — was essential: "To abandon them now that the place is overrun by miners would involve their destruction by more than a relapse into heathenism, namely in their being swallowed up in the miners' temptations to drink, gambling and immorality." The Klondike was for whites only; natives were welcomed only temporarily, as curiosities or suppliers of provisions and furs.

This isolation was not total, nor could it be, given the magnitude of the invasion. Natives along the routes leading to the Klondike found short-term work as labourers or guides. Many Indians in the Skagway area earned sizable sums packing supplies over the mountain passes. The development of new transportation systems, however, soon robbed them of this lucrative source of income. This advance in transporation also served to break the long-standing monopoly on inland trade held by the Tlingit, and freed interior natives from the military domination of the coastal Indians. The miners also brought disease, all but wiping out the natives near the Klondike, and spreading deadly illnesses throughout the territory.

A few natives sought a greater accommodation with the gold rush society. The co-discoverers, Tagish Charlie and Skookum Jim, took thousands of dollars out of their Bonanza Creek claims. Tagish Charlie sold his holdings in 1901 and retired to Carcross. He spent his fortune lavishly, but drank too much and died in 1908 when he fell off a bridge and drowned. Skookum Jim also had trouble coping with his wealth. Historian Morris Zaslow wrote that he "tired of trying to keep up with the whites, eventually withdrew to Carcross and the safety of the church-dominated environment where he, too, died in 1916." Others found work as guides, woodcutters, and crewmen on the steamships. Most jobs were seasonal; by working in the summer, Indians were free to continue harvesting pursuits through the fall and winter. In general, however, Indians found themselves on the periphery of the territorial order, a position they occupied through a combination of preference, missionary and police edict, and discriminatory measures on the part of the general population.

The gold rush also affected natives beyond the Yukon River valley, albeit in rather unexpected ways. News of gold discoveries on the shores of Great Slave Lake diverted some Klondike-bound prospectors heading out from Edmonton. The subsequent economic growth, plus some improvements to transportation systems in the upper Mackenzie region, foreshadowed further exploitation of the mineral, oil and fur wealth of the district. Eager to encourage economic activity in this potentially rich region, the federal government sought to remove native title to the land through a treaty. Government commissioners, aided by missionaries and the NWMP, collected signatures on a hastily drafted and poorly explained treaty. By 1899, Treaty 8 was in place. The document affected a huge district, much larger in fact than that canvassed by the government agents. The upper Mackenzie River valley, from Edmonton in the south to Great Slave Lake in the north, and from the middle of northern British Columbia to the east end of Lake Athabasca, was surrendered for development. A small appendage north from the 60th parallel to Great Slave Lake ensured that as yet unproven gold diggings were covered by the agreement.

The Yukon Indians were not offered a treaty, nor, for the time being, were the natives on the lower Mackenzie River. In this part of the Mackenzie River valley the settlement potential appeared minimal and the government saw little value in expending time and money on marginal lands. Somewhat similar logic applied in the Yukon. The discovery of gold indicated to some that the time for a treaty had come, but there was a strong reluctance to surrender potentially valuable land to the Indians. As government agent William Ogilvie said in response to a request for a reserve for the Moosehide band: "Discoveries of gold have been made in that vicinity and before I recommend any extension of the 160 acres, I will await the development of this grounds, as gold mining ground." In addition, the government remained convinced that the area could not sustain permanent development. When the gold was gone, the government reasoned, the people would leave. Hence, there was no reason to reserve land for the natives. The Indians made at least one overture concerning treaty rights, but it was firmly rebuffed.

The North After the Gold Rush

The north had been transformed. The old mining communities all but disappeared, and were replaced by Dawson, the entrepôt of Whitehorse at the foot of the White Horse rapids, and a string of other small centres which sprang up to serve the miners. But the rush itself lasted only a short time. Its fall was almost as rapid as its ascent. With most of the viable claims staked in the first few months, the thousands of newcomers could only wait restlessly for news of a new strike. Strikes in Atlin, British Columbia and the even larger field at Nome, Alaska in 1898 started the exodus, which began even as the rush to Dawson continued.

A reorganization of the mines, which saw large companies buy out many individual claim holders, signalled a turning point. By World War I, only two decades after the gold rush began, Dawson City had been reduced to a shell and the communities along the creeks had all but disappeared. The collapse of Dawson was not complete — the goldfields had passed into a new phase.

The post-gold rush society looked vaguely familiar, for it represented a return to the scale and pace of development of the pre-Klondike period. After, as before, the region was dominated by a single industry and a single town, the population was highly transient, and the federal government expressed marginal interest in an isolated district. The Klondike gold rush was an aberration, a sharp contrast with the past, but not a portent of the future. The regional order of the Yukon Territory and the neighbouring Northwest Territories rested on limited, small-scale developments, an active accommodation with the native population, and federal neglect of local concerns.

The Klondike era left a notable legacy. Although their perspectives tended to be short-term, both business and government expedited commercial innovations, which were designed to cash in on the rapid depletion of the gold resources. For the Canadian government, the chaos in the Yukon posed considerable difficulty, for authorities were forced to adapt quickly to novel situations. In short order, the government adopted a new administrative network, restructured constitutional arrangements and, reluctantly, began to chart the future of its northern districts.

There were other major changes as well. Transportation promoters paid particular attention to bottlenecks on the trail to the Klondike. As early as 1898, a hoist was in operation on the final slope of the Chilkoot Pass, and a small flotilla of sternwheelers plied the upper Yukon River. Entrepreneurs built tramways around Miles Canyon. On a larger scale, a railway was built from the coast to the navigable portion of the Yukon River. Men working their way to the goldfields provided much of the labour. When news of the Atlin strike in 1898 reached the railway crews, they deserted en masse and headed for the new Bonanza. In an era of massive government land and capital subsidies for railways, the White Pass and Yukon Route was built entirely with private capital.

The crush of people in the west-central Yukon demanded administrative changes. The government took the first step in 1895 when the Yukon was made a separate administrative "district" within the Northwest Territories. When the gold rush began, Inspector Constantine and the NWMP were the sole authorities in the Yukon. To support the Mounties, the federal government in 1898 dispatched the Yukon Field Force, a contingent of more than 200 Canadian army regulars ''whose presence was further evidence of the Canadian government's determination to hold the Yukon against subversion from within or attack from without.'' Other moves were taken to strengthen the federal administrative arm. The federal government appointed local officials, and so had established a more formal administration without major constitutional changes.

Appropriately, a debate over liquor taxes precipitated a re-assessment of the Yukon's legal status. The government of the Northwest Territories (then including Alberta, Saskatchewan, the Yukon, the current Northwest Territories, and additional districts) sent a delegate to the Yukon to enforce liquor regulations and collect taxes. The federal government also coveted these handsome revenues and passed the Yukon Territory Act (effective in 1898), establishing the Yukon as a distinct territorial unit subject to the administrative control of the federal government. An appointed commissioner, aided by an appointed council of other government officials, stood at the head of the new system. William Ogilvie, one of the few federal civil servants with northern experience, was appointed the first commissioner of the newly constituted district.

The establishment of the Yukon Territory gave formal shape to an emerging regional administration and simultaneously entrenched the district's colonial status. Since patronage was rife in the federal civil service, the new northern posts became depositories for favoured Liberal Party supporters (the Conservative Party's turn came in 1911, and they took full advantage of their opportunity). Because such patronage was accepted practice, few protested the arrangements, though the administration was rocked occasionally by scandals.

Local problems with the administration originated more with the structure than the exercise of power. Despite its vigour, the Yukon Territory remained under external control, subject to the whims of a distant federal government. Initially there was no provision for local representation in either the regional government or the federal House of Commons. Further, there was no intimation that changes were forthcoming.

The Yukon administration had been structured differently from the territorial administration then extant in the Northwest Territories. The head of government was named commissioner rather than lieutenant governor, a move which, according to historian L.H. Thomas, robbed "him of the powers and prestige of being the local representative of the Crown." This change, plus the absence of elected representation, demonstrated to Thomas that: "Irrespective of which party was in power in Ottawa there was a rooted aversion to popular democracy in the territories excused in this case by the presence of so many aliens in the population." It made sense in some ways to deny control to the largely American population in the Yukon, but the lack of responsible government was an affront to the miners.

The miners had several specific grievances, chiefly concerning royalty schedules and mining regulations, but resentment focused on the formalization of external control. As one historian noted,

> Political conflict is prevalent in every society, but where the environment is fluid, as it was in the Klon-

dike, this conflict becomes more intense. Because of the sweeping economic and social changes that beset the Yukon from 1898 to 1908, the region was a fertile breeding ground for discontent. The agitation that resulted was directed towards public authorities, who, many Yukoners believed, were capable of solving all problems once shown the proper means of approaching them.

Territorial opposition first emerged from several large miners' meetings called to protest federal actions. The local Conservative Party helped to crystallize the complaints, and their counterparts in Ottawa provided a national forum for the outcry from the far north. The people demanded greater local control; in particular, elected representation on a territorial council and two members in the House of Commons. Concessions came slowly and were granted with obvious reluctance. Voters were permitted to elect two members to territorial council in 1900, and two years later three additional elected positions were added. Also in 1902, Commissioner J.H. Ross announced that the territory would be granted a single seat in the House of Commons. The final step — toward representative, if not responsible, government — came in 1908 when an amendment to the Yukon Act provided for a wholly elected ten-member council.

A similar battle emerged at the civic level, where the territorial council administered the affairs of Dawson. The local citizenry were less than enthusiastic at the prospect of increased taxation, but agitation by leading politicians, including Commissioner Ross, led to the incorporation of Dawson City in 1901. These modest gains in local control came only after most of the ''Yankees'' had left and the population mix swung back in favour of British subjects.

The extension of electoral politics answered many of the miners' complaints, although constitutional arrangements ensured that the colonial relationship remained intact. Yukoners soon became adept at party, or machine, politics. The Liberals under Commissioner Frank Congdon built a formidable election machine, well-oiled by freely-dispensed patronage. The Conservatives organized as well, but their opposition status in national politics weakened their hand. The battle focused more on control of the ''pork barrel'' than political reform. The less than laudable stakes scarcely lessened the acrimony, and both political parties stooped to questionable tactics. Mrs. M. Black, wife of prominent Yukon Tory George Black, recalled the scandalous behaviour during a 1902 federal by-election:

> Numbers of foreigners were railroaded through a fake form of naturalization and allowed to vote....[Agents] gave Government supporters large credits on I.O.U.'s or 'Tabs' as they were called....After the election these were repudiated and unredeemed, and the party responsible and its followers nicknamed 'Tabs.' In one transaction the agent who went to Skagway with money to hire pluggers, lost his roll at the roulette wheel and had neither money nor tabs to pay the carload of imported aliens who, in the meantime, had voted. When they found that the agent had skipped the country, in their rage they smashed train windows, tore up seats and raised general ruction.

Access to patronage did not guarantee the Liberals success, and although they succeeded in placing J.H. Ross as the Yukon's first Member of Parliament, they fared less well in contests for territorial council seats. Because of the comparatively small population, political battles typically became intensely personal, and were won and lost on individual credibility, specific promises, and the ability to tap the simmering anti-Ottawa sentiment in the territory.

Even this limited apparatus of government carried costs, borne through property and liquor taxes and subsidized by federal grants. Territorial resource revenues were deposited in federal coffers. Limited financial resources restricted the territory's administrative capacity; the lack of qualified personnel, plus the low salaries offered to federal employees, forced the government to merge jobs. Thus many key people held both federal and territorial appointments. It also reinforced the appearance of colonial rule, blurring even further the already murky distinctions between regional and national governments.

Even with these structural difficulties and despite the slow decline of the Klondike goldfields, the Yukon Territory seemed to be advancing steadily toward responsible government. By 1908, the council sat at the pleasure of the electorate, although final authority still rested in the hands of the federally appointed Commissioner. Dawson City had full municipal institutions and the territory had an M.P. Yet the forms of responsible government only masked the realities of power, for the federal government, acting through the Minister of the Interior (Clifford Sifton, 1896-1905; Frank Oliver, 1905-1911), charted the territory's direction.

The gold rush caught the federal government unaware and suddenly responsible for an all but unknown district besieged by thousands of American prospectors. Clifford Sifton, the recently appointed Minister of the Interior, was a staunch promoter of western development and increased immigration, but he was ill-prepared to assume his northern responsibilities. Remedial measures, like establishing the Yukon Field Force, expanding the NWMP contingent, and taking preliminary administrative steps solved the immediate crisis but left the government without an overall policy. The minister, while personally excited about the northern developments, assigned the region second place behind his department's unwavering commitment to the settlement of the southern plains. Sifton was also convinced that the Yukon, for all its obvious wealth, had only modest prospects for permanent development.

His first priority was to ensure that a greater portion of the Klondike wealth flowed into Canadian hands. Most of the gold, mined by Americans and shipped through United States ports, provided little financial benefit for its country of origin. Sifton was not concerned about reinvestment in the Yukon; he wanted southern Canadian business and the federal government to get a greater share of the Klondike revenues. He tried to achieve this through some radical changes to the mining regulations. New laws reserved for the government every second claim on any newly opened creek and also imposed a heavy royalty on extracted gold. While perhaps laudable in intent, the measures indicated Sifton's lack of insight into northern conditions. The response was predictable. The *Klondike Miner* said of Sifton's maneuvers:

> A great deal has been said and written about the apparent lack of wisdom shown in the governing of this territory and in the laws and regulations under which we operate. After all is said and done does not the greater part of the trouble arise from the government of Canada attempting to keep this distant country directly under its own eye and control through local

officers who of very necessity, do not feel their
responsibility to the people of the locality as they do
to their own immediate superiors, the Dominion officials — the source of authority here.

The concerted opposition reported in the newspapers
and a series of mass meetings registered the public's
displeasure.

The royalty question, battles with the United States
over boundaries and customs regulations, regional
administrative difficulties, and the need for a long-
term policy for the district pulled the minister in several
directions simultaneously. Sifton visited the region
himself in 1897, hoping to resolve some of the
outstanding problems and mend an image tattered by
the debacle over mining regulations. His travels
convinced him of the need to offset American influence
in the goldfields.

Two measures — a reformed royalty package and
an all-Canadian water and rail link to circumvent United
States control of the mountain passes — emerged as
the cornerstone of the new, aggressive national policy.
They were deliberately short-term plans. Indeed they
were pursued with urgency because Sifton believed
the Yukon's glory days would soon be over. As he
wrote in August 1897, "The Yukon is not the same
as any other mining camp in the world and the difference consists in the fact that it is good for nothing
except mining, which in all probability will be temporary." The one person capable of forming government
policies to ensure permanent development believed the
effort to be fruitless.

The new policy was put into action quickly. The
key was a railway to be built by entrepreneurs William
Mackenzie and Donald Mann, linking the Stikine River

and Teslin Lake. From the latter point, just north of the Yukon-British Columbia border, steamships would provide access to the Klondike. Such a development would provide an all-Canadian alternative to the regular supply route through the Alaskan towns of Skagway and Dyea. The United States government, anxious to protect American business interests in the Klondike, countered Sifton's bold thrust by proposing wide-ranging legislative retaliation. The American opposition, coupled with obstruction of federal railway subsidies in the House of Commons by the Conservative Party, forced the government to back down. The U.S. government agreed to drop restrictions on Canadian goods passing through customs in exchange for the abandonment of the all-Canadian railway. Sifton's royalty policy similarly fell on hard times. His initial 20 per cent royalty dropped in a series of stages until, in 1902, the government removed royalty charges and imposed instead a 2 1/2 per cent export levy.

Before resigning as Minister of the Interior, Sifton also introduced sweeping and controversial changes in territorial mining regulations. Claims in the Klondike had been staked on an individual basis, although miners were permitted to accumulate land holdings. While publicly paying homage to this individualistic tradition, Sifton altered regulations to permit greater concentration of ownership and private control of the all-important water rights. The rationale for the move lay largely in the importation of new technology; massive dredges and hydraulic operations allowed for more systematic exploitation of the resource. The government decided to grant both large leases and water rights to corporations.

The new methods brought problems, not the least of which was the conflict between traditional placer-mining and the new corporate technology. The concession system also gave the government a marvelous patronage tool. While the Liberals suffered from the taint of corruption, the inexorable process of consolidation had started. Small holders gradually sold out to the corporations.

Sifton's various policies rested on the belief that the Yukon would enjoy but a short life; his legislation ensured that would be so. The Yukon Gold Company, inheritors of Treadgold's earlier developments, established itself as a major presence in the goldfields, using new hydraulic methods to scour the creek beds and hillsides for gold. The free miners were forced out, and they headed for active camps in Alaska and throughout the Canadian North. The concessionaires did more than change the mines. In short order, Dawson City had been transformed from a frontier boom-town to a supply town, more a company town than a vibrant gold rush community.

Dawson City and the Yukon goldfields did not collapse overnight. Klondike stories, by now embellished through the dramatic tales of Jack London and the poetry of Robert Service ensured that the stream of would-be prospectors would continue well into the century's second decade. Most stayed only a short time, particularly when they discovered that the only work in the territory seemed to be with the gold concessions and the White Pass and Yukon Route Transportation Company.

Signs of change still abounded. The railway from Skagway to Whitehorse and regular steamship service along the Yukon provided reliable and comparatively inexpensive transportation. A federally-operated telegraph system, in place by 1901, provided direct contact with the outside world. Small deposits of copper, coal, silver, and lead were developed, but none approached the scale of the Klondike fields.

Dawson City passed into a more staid existence as the free-spending miners left. Government agents, housed in several large and expensive administration buildings, gold company officials, labourers, and a few businessmen provided the only flesh remaining on the skeleton of what had earlier been the largest Canadian city west of Winnipeg.

It is tempting, and not altogether unjustifiable, to attribute the decline of the Yukon to the poor administration of the federal government. Clifford Sifton followed policies seemingly designed to limit the life of the territory. Where he did get involved, it was to head off an American challenge, or capture financial benefits for southern Canadian businessmen, friends of the Liberal Party and the federal government. His successor, Frank Oliver, proved more sympathetic to northern concerns during his tenure in office, but his elevation to the post of Minister of the Interior came after the crucial early phase in the development of the goldfields and well after national priorities had been set. The idea that the north should be exploited to the benefit of the south was scarcely new, for the development of the prairie west rested on similar assumptions. To convict Sifton and the Liberal administration of deliberate misconduct, however, is to put too much weight on their influence. Their actions merely reflected the prevailing view of the north.

The Yukon Territory technically possessed the resource potential for more regular development and settlement. Properly managed by an interventionist government, the wealth of the Klondike could have been reinvested in other regional resources, such as copper, silver, and timber. And the wealth generated in the goldfields was truly impressive. Peak production occurred in 1902-1903, when $12 million worth of gold was shipped out of the territory. One estimate places the total return from the Klondike fields at $250 million, most of it taken out after the introduction of concessions and dredges.

There were other reasons to believe that a more balanced and lasting economic base could have been built. Although it remained largely unproven, the region's agricultural capacity seemed capable of providing much of the food for a fairly large population. The use of local materials to support secondary industry would have added to these developments. While practically feasible, this scenario lacked one central ingredient (besides interventionist policy). Had there been a will to stay and to reinvest the rewards from the goldfields in the territory, further government assistance would not have been necessary. But the people, with a few exceptions, showed no great desire to stay. Over the years, the image of the north as an inhospitable — if wealthy — environment had become firmly entrenched. Federal officials shared this impression of the north and patterned their legislation accordingly. An integrated, stable society was technically possible, but the necessary public commitment and faith in the future was nonexistent.

By 1911, the pattern had been set. The federal census of that year revealed that Dawson City held only 2,500 people, a far cry from the glory days of the Klondike. Whitehorse remained only a small way-station, its population swelling in the summer as the transportation system moved into high gear, but contracting in the winter months. The earlier fur trade had not been destroyed, but with attention focused on the gold rush, it faded into the background. The territorial society became a seasonal society, abandoned each winter by those wealthy enough to leave or too poor to stay. It seemed as though the pessimistic forecasts of Clifford Sifton and others had indeed come true.

4
The Doldrums in the Middle North

As the prospectors and speculators abandoned the Klondike goldfields, the north receded from national consciousness. The decline was gradual and never total. But nostalgia had replaced a sense of potential; the supposed land of the future had become a land of the permanent past.

The years between 1905 and 1939 are crucial to an understanding of the region. A long-term view of the history of the north reveals that the booms were temporary, the busts never as complete as the myths suggest. Instead, conditions before the gold rush and during the post-Klondike phase reflect more accurately the pace and substance of northern development. The most consistent features of northern society were limited growth, federal government neglect, dependence on a small number of mines, a vibrant fur trade and a bicultural society. The decline of the Klondike was therefore more a return to normal than a collapse, more a retreat into an isolated, small-scale society rather than a slide into oblivion.

The Mining Economy

Mining remained the cornerstone of the regional economy. Massive dredges ate their way along the creek beds, depositing mounds of processed rock in their wake. On the hillsides, hydraulic operators washed gold-bearing dirt into large sluice boxes, continuing the destruction of the landscape. The technologically efficient operations stood in stark contrast to earlier systems; and the corporations that owned them were a sharp departure from the individualistic prospectors who opened the fields. The Klondike remained moderately prosperous, enough at least to support the small service and government centre left behind. But organization had replaced the chaos of the gold rush. The town of Dawson was joined to the creeks by a series of roads and a small railway, which operated between 1906 and 1914. Power plants built for the mines also provided electricity for Dawson. Tourists following the famous "Trail of 98" found a vastly different community than legend had led them to expect.

The dredges were efficient, but technology could not overcome resource depletion. Returns from the goldfields dwindled steadily. Gold production, which reached more than one million ounces in 1900, fell to 211,000 by 1910. By 1920 territorial production stood at only 73,000 ounces. Returns fluctuated until 1940, dropping as low as 26,000 ounces in 1926 and climbing to 88,000 ounces in 1939. Even more telling was the fact that the Klondike's share of Canadian gold production plummeted from 80 per cent in 1900 to 1.1 per cent in 1935.

Obviously, gold would not longer carry the territory. Even during the Klondike rush, however, prospectors had found other mineral deposits. Some of the effort bore fruit. Miners identified a major copper belt in the Whitehorse area, although high transportation costs and low commodity prices undermined early attempts to exploit the resource. The discovery of small patches of high-grade silver ore in the Tagish area generated short-term development. These finds, coupled with the continued search for another Bonanza, ensured that mining remained dominant.

The discovery of a silver/lead deposit near Mayo in 1906 promised to decisively break the dependence on gold. Transportation problems along the Stewart River detracted from the strike until the introduction of shallow-draught steamers. By 1914, commercial operations were in full swing, linked to external markets by a system of steamboats and the White Pass and Yukon Route railway.

The Yukon Gold Company dominated the new mining field. Given the high risks of frontier mining, the access to capital and contacts with potential markets offered by the large companies were essential to success. It meant, however, that a small group of companies — the gold concessionaires, the Elsa-Keno mining companies, and the White Pass and Yukon Route — controlled the territory.

Resource-based economies are always vulnerable to external market forces, and the Yukon was no exception. For a time, improvements in world mineral prices encouraged an expansion in mining. The high transportation costs which had strangled earlier attempts to develop the Whitehorse copper fields were temporarily overcome by abnormally high prices for the ore. Operations expanded accordingly, so much so that during World War I the functioning mines had difficulty finding enough miners. With gold, silver/lead, and copper mines in production, the territory enjoyed a spurt of surprising prosperity. When the war ended, markets collapsed and several mines closed. Copper production ceased entirely, and only the discovery of rich new veins of ore in the Mayo district saved local mines.

Continuing high silver prices encouraged further developments in the Mayo-Keno area. Treadwell Yukon Company, for example, bought up several small operations, expanded its mining program and, in 1924, built a concentrating mill. By the mid-1920s, the silver/lead mines were carrying the Yukon, replacing the Klondike gold companies as the territory's economic cornerstone. Meanwhile, in the goldfields, ownership became increasingly concentrated in the hands of fewer companies. New dredges, improved hydraulic techniques and steam-thawing procedures (to permit longer periods of operation in the permanently frozen gravel) cost money, far more than was available to any small operator. In 1929, several medium-sized companies merged into the Yukon Consolidated Gold Corporation, a major union of capital, technical expertise and property holdings.

The technological improvements and the move to ever greater concentration of ownership only underscored the central malaise of the Yukon gold industry. Yields fell dramatically, costs continued to rise, and gold prices remained low. The federal government again altered mining regulations in a continuing attempt to assist the large corporations in their conquest of the creeks. Government aid, however, seldom moved beyond legislative changes, with the exception of small subsidies to encourage prospecting in undeveloped areas.

The cycles continued into the next decade. The Keno Hill mines suffered from low prices, although the losses here were partially offset by the richness of the ore. But the veins were quickly depleted and several times in the 1930s it appeared that the entire operation — mines, concentrating mill, and Stewart River steamships — would close. Treadwell Yukon Company rebounded, reopening several old shafts, and uncovering in the process rich deposits which allowed its operations to continue. From the beginning, the exceptionally high-quality ores in the Keno-Elsa area had offset often unfavourable world market conditions and extreme transportation difficulties.

The depression years, ironically, also instigated renewed activity in the goldfields. In the midst of the general economic collapse, the price of gold jumped from slightly more than $21 an ounce in 1931 to more than $35 an ounce four years later. Yukon producers responded rapidly to the improved conditions. Annual territorial output increased from around 40,000 fine ounces in the early 1930s to more than 80,000 fine ounces by the end of the decade.

Many young men unable to find work in the south came north to the goldfields. The unusual and unexpected labour surplus allowed the dredging companies to expand operations. Many of these early developments were carried out on the backs of the workers, who paid dearly for the luxury of a job. Worker protests could not be stayed forever, though, and as accusations of improper treatment mounted, particularly against the Yukon Consolidated Gold Company, modest improvements in wages and living conditions were provided. In this atmosphere of unexpected prosperity, new dredges were added and additional warehouse space built. Even so, these developments scarcely constituted a boom, and expansion proceeded with a caution instilled by earlier crashes. Gold had, however, won back its place in the territorial order.

The renewed vigour of northern mining proved only a modest lure to the fortune-hunters. In the case of existing mines, the established companies passed few of their profits on to the workmen. Even prospecting had become somewhat more difficult, as hard times limited the money available to outfit prospectors. A few came north of their own accord, often combining trapping and trading with prospecting. Most, however, came with the backing of national mining companies, like the powerful Consolidated Mining and Smelting Company (Cominco), and could maintain operations only as long as the parent company remained interested. This expanded activity pushed beyond the borders of the familiar Yukon Territory into the Mackenzie River valley.

The Mackenzie region's potential had long been in question, highlighted by a flurry of interest in the Great Slave Lake area. Those small gold discoveries continued to draw prospectors. The work was rewarded, and in 1935 a small rush to the Yellowknife area established the gold industry on a more permanent footing. By the end of the 1930s, several small mines operated along the north shore of Great Slave Lake. Signs of extensive ore-bodies pointed to an even more profitable future.

Miners struck more than gold as they prospected in the Mackenzie River drainage basin. Years earlier, before the Klondike gold rush, native guides had shown fur traders oil seepages along the banks of the Mackenzie River. In August 1920, an Imperial Oil crew struck oil at Norman Wells, inspiring grandiose predictions of an oil boom on the northern frontier. Distance and cost kept developments to a minimum, with production only for local markets. Expanding mining operations in the 1930s led to increased demand. That in turn convinced Imperial Oil to upgrade its small refinery. The oil industry was developed more slowly than gold; the potential had been identified, modest improvements had "proven" the field, but full-scale production remained some years off.

Gordon LaBine uncovered yet another prize, this time along the wind-blown shores of Great Bear Lake, when he found pitchblende (radium-bearing ore) at Port Radium. Medical investigations by the Curies had demonstrated the usefulness of radium (extracted from ore only after a difficult and costly process) in combatting cancer. Demand for the high-grade Mackenzie district radium, consequently, was high. Although costs appeared prohibitive, and transportation problems interfered with production, private capital and government assistance put a mine into operation. The immense distance between Port Radium and LaBine's refinery in Port Credit, Ontario, necessitated the use of aircraft to ship the ore.

On the whole, the mining developments in the north were scattered and far from spectacular. High-grade ores at Keno Hill and Port Radium rated immediate development, but the exceptionally high production costs kept excitement to a minimum. Gold production had expanded, particularly in the Great Slave Lake area. But here, operators recognized the tenuous nature of their business and proceeded with caution. These developments between the gold rush and 1939 represented the north's more natural course of growth. Mines received little if any government encouragement. The mining companies, reporting to "outside" shareholders, responded to the vagaries of world market conditions and the high costs of northern development by "high grading" the ore — taking what was easily accessible or demonstrably profitable while avoiding commitments to marginal properties. As a result, the territories hosted a cyclical mining economy, often seasonal, supporting only a small, largely transient, and male population.

The northern transportation network expanded to serve the mining industry. By the late 1920s, air mail service had been extended to the Yukon and in 1937 Edmonton and Whitehorse were connected by regular commercial flights. Yet riverboats remained the key to northern transportation. The extensive Yukon system underwent modest expansion as lighter and faster vessels were added to allow for an extension of service to isolated districts. In the Mackenzie River district, a network had to be erected on the foundation established earlier by the HBC. Such companies as the Mackenzie River Transportation Company and the Northern Transportation Company (taken over by Eldorado Gold Mining Company in 1937) carried supplies to the new mining camps along Great Bear and Great Slave Lakes. Air transport also played a major role, as charter aircraft companies began ferrying both men and supplies to the mines, and carrying ore to market.

These improvements in transportation and the modest expansion of the northern economy did not ignite new interest in the region. The hesitation of northern businessmen was noted in southern quarters. The limited mining development between the gold rush and World War II demonstrated to many Canadians that the government had been right; there would be no permanence on the northern mining frontier. That suitable government assistance might have aided developments (as railway subsidies did for the prairies, northern Ontario, and British Columbia) seemed not to register.

The Fur Trade

While mining rested in the doldrums, periodically awakened by new discoveries, the fur trade maintained a modest pace of activity, occasionally rising to periods of spectacular growth. There was no rapid decline as there had been in the south beginning in 1870. Instead, the fur trade flourished during and after the gold rush, although the higher profile accorded the gold stampede drew attention away from the stable, but no longer exotic, fur industry. The fur trade remained a central feature of the northern economy after World War I, continuing to draw natives and whites together in an economic and social setting that was both creative and destructive.

Because the industry was labour (rather than capital) intensive, many more people in the north were involved with the harvesting and exchange of furs than with mining. The annual returns from the northern fur trade often rivalled those from the mines. In 1921, the Yukon and Northwest Territories exported slightly more than $1.7 million in minerals; that same year (1921-1922), some $2 million in furs were shipped south. Ten years later, the figures were $2.2 million and $2.1 million respectively. In other years, however, mining profits far outstripped those of fur trading.

Like mining, the fur trade was sensitive to external markets, specifically those set in the halls of high fashion. In the 1920s, for example, a sharp rise in the price of silver fox pelts fueled a peak period of prosperity in the northern trade. The marketing of furs involved a more complex procedure than did the distribution of ore concentrate. Numerous middlemen handled the furs between the native trappers and the fur salons. In the north, trappers often had a choice of several trading companies. The furs then passed through a wholesaler to fur auctions in the south. Purchasers selected pelts of species and quality to suit their particular needs, most of which related to formal fashion wear. Profits were extracted at each stage, ensuring that only a much whittled portion of the final selling price actually returned to the trappers.

The fur trade had also changed from an industry largely under the control of the HBC to a more competitive enterprise. Price fluctuations and high business costs in the north imposed their own limits, however, giving a perpetual edge to the larger, integrated companies. Although the competition between independents and large firms was strong, the more substantial firms emerged very much in control by 1940.

The Yukon trade remained more competitive than that in the Northwest Territories. The withdrawal of the HBC just before the gold rush had opened the district to American traders. As Canadian businessmen gained control from the Americans when the Klondike developments declined, the industry underwent some notable changes. The number of traders operating each year varied widely, according to the profitability of the trade. When prices rose, independent operators entered the fray.

The Taylor and Drury Company dominated the Yukon trade. In 1921 the company ran a string of seven posts scattered throughout the territory. New posts opened and old ones closed, but the firm had little difficulty keeping its two steamers, *Thistle* and *Yukon Rose*, active. The HBC re-entered the territory several times, but the numerous independent traders represented the greatest challenge to Taylor and Drury. In 1930, the territorial government granted licences for forty separate posts. The smaller operations proved particularly vulnerable to market forces, and many closed after only a few years. Their mere existence, however, kept the larger companies from taking undue advantage of their economic strength.

Further east, in the Mackenzie River district, a re-invigorated fur trade maintained its pre-eminence. It proved, however, to be vastly different from the pre-gold rush era, when the HBC dominated the industry. The transition from HBC monopoly to competitive trade was far from immediate, for the Company marshalled impressive financial resources and its solid northern experience to fend off poorly prepared newcomers.

Competition initially focused on the larger native communities. A few companies like Hislop and Nagle (later Northern Traders Ltd.) established a string of posts paired with HBC establishments. A sharp escalation in fur prices in the 1910s and 1920s spurred others to try their hand at the trade. The Mackenzie River valley received the bulk of these newcomers; between 1920 and 1924, over seventy posts operated at twenty locations from Great Slave Lake to the Mackenzie delta. Intense competition forced others to push into the back country. The Alberta-based Northern Trading Company, Lamson and Hubbard Canadian Company and, in the Keewatin district, the French firm Révillion Frères, chipped away at the HBC's dominance. Independents proved even more mobile, although they often depended on the larger companies both for supplies and a market for their furs. Competition, with attending high prices, generous bonuses, readily available credit, and other enticements, hit a fever pitch, as traders rushed to meet the native trappers in their camps before they reached the trading centres. This practice, called ''tripping,'' clearly favoured the small, mobile traders in their contest with the larger firms. The HBC, a favourite of the federal government, appealed for official intervention, and in

1929 regulations prohibiting such operations were passed.

Fur trade competition peaked by 1930. The HBC had managed to retain its leadership position, but not without a significant drop in profits. At the same time, the intense competition that had spread throughout the Mackenzie River valley and well into the back country had produced a major reduction in the fur resource. The larger companies, particularly the HBC, increasingly subsidized their native trappers, providing sufficient food and supplies on credit to keep them in the field even though trapping was no longer profitable. The onset of the Great Depression, ravaging fur markets in the south, hastened the decline in the trade. Prices and demand collapsed, forcing a severe rationalization of the trade.

As the largest company in the north, the HBC easily weathered the storm. But most small operators dropped out, with those who remained supporting themselves by personal trapping. Even the larger competitors gradually abandoned the trade. One by one, Lamson and Hubbard (1924), Révillion Frères (1936) and Northern Trading Company (1938) sold out to the HBC. The HBC could not count on a complete monopoly, but as the principal supplier and marketing agency for the independents, it had regained its dominance of the Mackenzie River trade. The government assisted the rationalization of the trade in 1938, restricting trapping licences to natives and whites already in the north. This move was designed to discourage unprepared southerners from seeking to make it rich in the sub-Arctic trade.

The changing structure of the fur trade did not lessen the industry's hold on the regional economy. Most major settlements centred on trading posts; the fur companies owned and operated the principal transportation systems; and most people made their living from the trade. Unlike the Yukon, where dredging operations and silver/lead mining overshadowed a resurgent fur trade, in the Northwest Territories the industry maintained its pre-eminence. Only at the end of the 1930s did the balance begin to shift, following mineral discoveries near Great Bear and Great Slave Lakes. The fur trade survived after 1940, but as in the Yukon, it would be shunted from the limelight by the more intensive and, to southerners, more interesting mining operations.

The continuation of the fur trade offered natives a modest opportunity to determine their level of participation in the northern Canadian economy. Although a number of Indians, primarily in the Yukon, found seasonal work in the mines or with the transportation companies, most continued to hunt and trap, an option that was both culturally preferable and economically logical. Given the racial discrimination endemic in the mines and the fluctuations of activity in the extractive industries, the fur trade remained the most obvious commercial undertaking. Trapping and market hunting were often combined with cutting wood for the steamboats or other such seasonal activities. Together, these pursuits allowed the natives to meet their needs for southern manufactured goods. They were particularly interested in such items as outboard motors (which expanded their trapping range and reduced travel time), steel traps, and better rifles.

There were problems with the white "bushmen" who entered the north in the 1920s and 1930s. The natives had not always husbanded the fur resources carefully, but their harvesting practices were much more cautious than those of the bushmen. The whites were seldom committed to the region and, hoping to earn enough money to return south or to enter a different business, they often over-trapped and invaded Indian hunting territories. This in turn generated considerable resentment among the native people (particularly as the officers of the RNWMP were often slow in responding to native complaints).

D.J. Murdoff, Assistant General Manager for The Northern Trading Company at Fort Resolution, offered one of the best descriptions available of the impact of this modest 'invasion:'

> Last year the influx of trappers was so great that in some sections, there is a very grave danger that the animals will become extinct in a very short time. Between Resolution and Smith we have no less than fifty-five white trappers (a trapper for every three miles) so you can get some idea how devoid of game this district will be after this winter. Heretofore this territory has been supporting ten to fifteen families from year to year, but this winter they have all been forced to abandon their homes and seek other trapping grounds. The inevitable outcome of this influx will be that the country will soon be trapped out, the Indian destitute, with no means of supporting himself. The Government will be compelled to feed and cloth[e] the whole population....Another very objectionable feature is the class of trappers this year; with few exceptions, they are a collection of the riff raff from outside, without capital or means.

The fur trade had changed in other ways as well. Before the gold rush, the newness of the northern trade left the natives in an advantageous position. Their material needs were limited and changed slowly. However, by the twentieth century, new technology had supplanted traditional tools, clothing, and weaponry, and eroded many traditional skills. The Indians became increasingly dependent on manufactured goods, a dependence heightened by the extensive use of credit designed to tie hunters to a trading post and keep them in the field. There was little altruism in the granting of credit. Anglican missionary C.C. Brett noted that the Indians of Teslin ''will be in need of relief about Xmas. Taylor and Drury have cut off their credit entirely, as they conduct business to suit themselves and Mr. Drury told me that 'they weren't running a benevolent society for the Indians.' '' Not all companies acted in this fashion. The HBC, for example, offered relief to the aged and indigent from almost all their posts, performing a task emblematic of their quasi-state role in the north. The Company, of course, applied for and received compensation for such expenses from the Department of Indian Affairs. The changes in the structure of the fur trade meant that by the 1940s many natives had been drawn into greater dependence on the trade, often relying on the post for both food and material goods.

There were some opportunities for natives besides the fur trade — moreso in the Yukon than in the Mackenzie River district where alternatives opened up more slowly and were more often dominated by whites. Klondike publicity had had its effect, and tourism increased in importance through the 1920s and 1930s. Big-game hunting became a prominent branch of this new enterprise. Reports of trophy-size moose, caribou, and sheep caught the attention of southern sportsmen. Indians understandably found a ready niche in this new industry, although discriminatory government measures barred them from holding licences as chief guides. Although such a licence had been granted to Johnny

Johns, the most famous of Yukon guides, subsequent applications were rejected.

Harvesting skills proved useful for more than guiding a southern "greenhorn" to an acceptable kill. The mining camps and settlements needed fresh meat, and until a change in government regulations in the 1940s suspended such sales, natives regularly sold moose and caribou carcasses. Fish could also be sold profitably in most towns. In each instance, these alternative opportunities provided a supplement to, instead of a replacement for, more regular harvesting practices. Natives remained preoccupied with the fur trade, and found little room for participation in the mining economy.

. The northern economy consisted of two distinct sectors. Mining was dominated by transient white workmen employed by a number of large, externally-controlled corporations. Natives seldom appeared in the mining camps. While the fur trade was also mainly in the hands of a few companies, it depended upon native workers, and the companies had to be at least partially sympathetic to Indian needs. Over time, the companies drew the natives into increasing reliance on the trading posts, but until the 1940s the trade remained generally remunerative and culturally acceptable.

Society in the Middle North

The obvious economic division — between the Yukon and the Northwest Territories and between the mining camps and the fur trading centres — created social distinctions. People were drawn together for particular tasks, but kept apart by strong economic, social, and cultural forces. Like the economy, northern society during the post-gold rush years returned to earlier patterns. Once the wave of prospectors, prostitutes, and camp followers passed through, the native people regained some of their numerical significance. The fur trade social pattern re-emerged in many parts of the north, but a residue of the separate white society remained very much in evidence.

Canadian society had not dealt kindly with native people through the first decades of the twentieth century. A preoccupation with economic development and agricultural settlement — progress in all possible forms — had resulted in the shunting aside of native people. The natives were relegated to reserves, where they suffered the ravages of economic deprivation, increasing abuse of alcohol, and the continued toll of alien diseases. A still-surviving attitude of paternalism convinced the Christian churches and the federal government that the attempt to "civilize" the natives had to continue. This often occurred through residential schools, which forced prolonged and painful separation of parents and children. The Canadian people seemed more concerned with administering the native "problem," as it was so readily called, than with providing a future for the aboriginal people. There were few efforts on a national scale to protect or replace the harvesting lifestyle that, in southern districts, was no longer viable. Natives seemed to have been cut adrift; even the apparent protection of the negotiated treaties did little to assist the Indians with their often difficult transition to a very different new world.

This general national pattern was not repeated directly in northern districts. So long as the harvesting economy remained economically viable, natives were able to ignore or overcome discrimination, legislative barriers and economic upheaval. Throughout much of the north, however, the dislocation, extensive alcohol abuse, and loss of esteem which seemed to characterize native people across the country had not yet taken firm hold. But it was not possible to avoid entirely the imperatives of the new age.

There were areas where natives were clearly not desired. Whitehorse, Dawson City, and the mining camps remained white preserves. Natives came only to sell fish and meat or trade furs, to visit government officials, and (illegally) buy liquor. Formal and informal discrimination encouraged the Indians to keep their visits brief. The federal government laid out small native residential reserves near, but separate from the white communities. Superintendent Moodie of the RNWMP reported in 1913 that the Indians in Whitehorse ''are kept out of town as much as possible, but it is only by bluff.'' Although the measures were obviously *ultra vires*, Indian Agent John Hawksley and police officers imposed curfews and established a permit system in the 1930s to regulate native access to Dawson and Whitehorse.

The white population was also remarkably transient. Each year, the lure of the Klondike played its magic, drawing people north in search of their own Eldorado. Just as regularly, the region exacted its toll and many left, often scrambling to catch the last sternwheelers in order to quit the territories before the rivers froze. Because of its role as an entrepôt between rail and river, Whitehorse was particularly vulnerable to seasonal migrations. Workers and businessmen left each year as the ice set and returned with spring break-up. Thus the town was left with a skeletal population in winter, which easily trebled in size during the hectic summer season. Dawson City experienced similar, if less dramatic, swings, since its role as territorial capital and regional supply centre kept more people on site year-round.

Yukon society was, physically at least, extremely isolated from southern culture and life. Although the Dominion Telegraph reached Dawson City by 1901, the vast distances imposed an impressive psychological barrier. It was a barrier that northern residents resisted in a constant battle to stay abreast of world events. National and international news dominated the Dawson newspapers, and even the more parochial weekly, the Whitehorse *Star*, offered regular coverage of external happenings. The outbreak of war in Europe in 1914 provided a major test of the region's distance from reality.

The war presented an interesting challenge to the small population in the Yukon Territory. With the battlefields thousands of miles away, the confrontation lacked immediacy and relevance. Yukoners could easily have hidden behind the cloak of isolation and ignored the war. They did no such thing. Martha Black, wife of the Commissioner of the Yukon, described the response of the audience at a Dawson theatre to the news of the declaration of war:

> As though answering an overwhelming urge, they stood in unison and commenced to sing 'God Save the King.' The effect was electrical. With one move, the audience was on its feet, and never in the world, I dare say, was our national anthem sung with greater fervour or more depth of feeling than in that moving picture house in that little town on the rim of the Arctic. Although eight thousand miles of mountain, land and sea separated us from London, the heart of the Empire, yet England's King was our King, and England's Empire was our Empire.

Yukoners followed the war with passionate interest, desperate to demonstrate their involvement in the country's battles. They echoed the nationalistic rhetoric spewing out of Ottawa. With a population over 60 per cent British and Canadian, the enthusiasm made sense; it was the intensity that was unusual. Within months, hundreds of young men headed south to enlist. Gold tycoon Joe Boyle organized and outfitted a machine gun company, a patriotic exercise which cost some $50,000. Yukon Commissioner George Black followed Boyle's lead and in 1916 led the 260 men of the Yukon Infantry (17th Machine Gun Company) off to war. Still others left to work in southern war industries, creating a manpower drain which hampered mining efforts in the Klondike creeks.

Those who remained behind did not let the war pass them by. News from the front filled the local newspapers, particularly when territorial units reached the battle-lines. Contributions flowed into the coffers of patriotic organizations. It became a matter of intense regional pride that territorial donations far outstripped, on a per capita basis, national and provincial averages. Like other Canadians, many Yukoners came to view the war as one for moral purity and social improvement as well as military victory over the enemy. The battle for prohibition of alcohol gave Canadians an opportunity to justify the sacrifices overseas, and a solid core of Yukoners joined the fight. They lost the referendum battle (not surprisingly in the miner-dominated region), but that they came within three votes of winning suggests a strenuous effort to improve the Yukon for the boys "over there."

This war effort, ironically, almost proved to be the Yukon's undoing. While struggling to prove their importance to the nation, Yukoners actually heightened their vulnerability. The exodus of young men drained the pool of available labour, increased wage rates, and hampered mining ventures. With gold production down more then 50 per cent from 1914 to 1918, and with a consequent decline in government revenues, it appeared as though the territorial economy was on its last legs. The population fell by more than 50 per cent from pre-war figures. Dawson City, formerly a boom town of over 20,000, could count only 800 residents in 1921. But the final blow, one that symbolized the tenuous balance of white society in the Yukon, was still to come.

Each fall, many of the well-heeled citizens of Dawson and Whitehorse headed south for warmer climates. In October 1918, 343 passengers and crew (many Yukon residents), boarded the *Princess Sophia* at Skagway for a trip to Vancouver. That night, in the midst of a bitter fall storm, the ship ran aground. Daylight revealed the *Princess Sophia* caught on a reef, with several ships anchored alongside ready to take off passengers. The captain refused, and convinced those on board he would soon free his vessel. For another day, the ships stood close by, waiting for permission to move in. It never came. Another evening gale dragged the ship's bottom over the reef; the hull split and all on board were lost. The passenger list included many leading citizens of Dawson and Whitehorse. The loss of so many friends and business leaders was a harsh blow for a territory already ravaged by the social costs of a distant war.

New developments in the mining industry ensured some measure of permanence to the Yukon communities, but the Yukon between World War I and World War II seemed to have imploded, shrinking to a shadow of the Klondike glory days. The main towns and mining camps retained their white-only character, but they were much smaller than before. The changes brought some signs of stability as well, although the decline from earlier heights made stability look curiously like rigor mortis. The population remained generally constant, aided by the depression when few left jobs in the north for non-existent opportunities elsewhere. The population also became more sexually balanced. In 1901, the ratio of males to females stood at 572:100; by 1931, the ratio had fallen to 202:100. The imbalance still illustrated the single-male orientation of the northern mining frontier, but the Yukon was taking on a more "settled" air, with government offices and churches gradually replacing the gambling halls and brothels.

In the back country, not much had changed from earlier patterns. The economic interdependence of natives and whites ensured extensive personal contact, reflected in short-term liaisons or marriages between traders and Indian women. The more settled members of white society looked down on the "squaw men." Laura Berton told a sad tale of one man:

> She was a pretty little thing, bright and neat, and I think could have made him a good wife, but the parents were so shocked they would neither see nor speak with him. This attitude drove him from the town and back into the bush, where his life was spent among the Indians, hunting and cutting wood for a living. Now here he was, standing by the river with his dark, wiry children clustered about him, the fish wheel in the background turning slowly with the current, the salmon smoking under the trees. In all intents and purposes he was a native.

This disapproval notwithstanding, the fur trade social order enjoyed greater stability than did the mining camps.

The back country was not free from tensions, particularly during the 1920s and 1930s when white "bushmen" arrived in substantial numbers. Problems typically involved accusations of over-killing of game by natives or use of poisons by whites. The RNWMP fretted constantly about violence, but few flare-ups actually occurred. The police were still kept busy, largely in an ultimately fruitless attempt to control the use of alcohol. Though the federal government prohibited native people in Canada from buying or consuming alcohol, such restrictions proved extremely difficult to enforce in the sparsely populated Yukon. White bootleggers earned a handsome profit, at minimal risk, for helping Indians circumvent police surveillance. The RNWMP tried to stem the flow of liquor, although their commitment to the cause rested more on a stereotyped notion of the Indians debauched by booze than on a realistic assessment of the effects of native drinking in this area. Notably, attempts to stop the flow of liquor represented almost the sum total of the force's Indian work.

Social conditions in the sub-Arctic regions of the Northwest Territories paralleled those in the Yukon. The emerging mining camps were dominated by transient white male workers who moved easily from mine to mine as diggings played out and new prospects were uncovered. With the introduction of bush planes, the "sojourner" character of the frontier miner became even more evident. Southern investors organized the capital for a survey, hired men in staging centres like Edmonton or Saskatoon, and shipped crew and supplies to a likely site. Contact with the native population was minimal, except when Indians came to the camps to sell meat or fish. The small towns which sprung up around major strikes, like Port Radium or Yellowknife, were rough places dominated by single men, with liquor and a few prostitutes thrown in for recreation. After the claims proved their worth, some men brought wives and families north, quickly adding a different cast to camp life. Most of the mining towns were small — 100 to 200 men.

The fur trade social order predominated throughout the Northwest Territories. Substantial fur trade settlements developed, usually around an old HBC post like Fort Simpson, Fort Providence, Fort Good Hope and Fort McPherson. The concentration of competitive traders, missionaries, and Mounted Police officers at any of these locations encouraged natives to gather, if only on a seasonal basis. It was not much removed from the nineteenth century fur trade order, except that the deluge of white traders, trappers, and agents added variety and competition to the former HBC system.

The Federal Government and Northern Natives

While the missionaries (Anglicans in the Yukon and both Anglicans and Catholics in the Mackenzie River valley) continued their efforts to recast native attitudes and lifestyle, the federal government adopted a more laissez-faire approach. The high cost of extending services to the north and the limited white presence there convinced federal officials that the Indians were best left as Indians. Despite the pious pronouncements of the Indian Act, which called for the assimilation and "civilization" of the natives, the government felt little compulsion to follow through. As Frank Pedley, Deputy Superintendent General of Indian Affairs wrote in 1906, "I think we should have a definite policy that the aborigines north of that line [60th parallel] should not be brought into treaty but that Indian affairs should be administered in that far northern country as the needs of the case suggest.'' Rather than offering treaties, the federal government tried, after a fashion, to support the natives in their role as harvesters. The decision rested more on a desire to limit federal spending than on a belief in the value of the native lifestyle.

Since there was no treaty in the Yukon, the government operated with a free hand. Although wanting to keep the natives on the trapline, federal officials rebuffed all efforts to reserve specific land for Indian use. As Charles Camsell, deputy minister of the Department of Mines, argued:

> If we are not going to reserve our northern regions exclusively for the use of the natives but are looking to encourage the opening of these regions to the people of Canada generally, then I think we must limit the extent of the preserves to meet the pressing needs of the natives but no more.

While shying away from permanent measures, the government did provide a fairly broad medical programme (including professional advice, hospital care and free medication for those in need who presented themselves to government agents in the towns). The appointment of former Anglican missionary John Hawksley as Indian Agent in 1914 regularized these federal initiatives, but since he seldom ventured from his Dawson City base, the government continued to rely on police and clergy to deliver most services.

A similarly modest programme operated in the Mackenzie River valley, again relying on the police. With many whites entering the southern Mackenzie region in the 1910s, the government felt greater supervision of native-white affairs was called for. In 1911,

Indian Agents were placed at Fort Smith (inside the boundary of Treaty 8) and Fort Simpson. By the 1930s, new agencies had been opened at Fort Resolution and Fort Good Hope. As in the Yukon, government services remained limited to emergency medical care and short-term relief in times of economic distress. In 1939-40, when the native population of the Northwest Territories stood at 3,700, federal expenditures totaled $43,000 for medical care and $24,000 for welfare — neither a princely sum.

The missionaries vigorously protested the government's "hands-off" approach and demanded greater support for their programme of Christianization and civilization. Civil servants and politicians in Ottawa did not share the missionaries' enthusiasm, but felt compelled for political reasons to assist the work of the "wilderness saints." Education emerged as the cornerstone of weak federal assistance to clerical plans for native "improvement."

Faced with incessant appeals from missionaries, the government reluctantly funded both day and residential schools, although it held little hope that either would be of much benefit. The day schools, referred to by one federal official as "a very imperfect means of education," proved ineffective. Native mobility limited the time children spent in school to a few months each summer. The scattered mission stations were poorly staffed, often with recent recruits who had few relevant linguistic or cultural skills. (This was less of a problem for the more permanent Catholic clergy.) In the Yukon, a chain of irregularly maintained and poorly attended seasonal schools operated in conjunction with the Anglican missions. Less effort was expended by the churches in the Mackenzie district.

Residential schools were more important to both missionaries and the government. The boarding schools were often imposing structures, complete with dormitories, classrooms and training facilities. To the missionaries, such schools offered the best hope for the nomadic Indians of the north. Children would be removed from the "backward" influences of family and community and given language, moral, Christian, and vocational training sufficient for full participation in the white world. A realistic appraisal of the limited prospects for northern development convinced most school principals to alter their training programmes to suit regional opportunities. The limited emphasis on relevant job skills did not, however, mask the fact that the teachers hoped to make major changes in hygiene, social behaviour, and work habits. It was hoped that graduates would re-enter their communities as disciples of a new Christian social order, assisting in the social "improvement" of the entire native population.

Although missionaries placed great emphasis on their "success" stories, the general experience of the students in their "afterlife" was far from positive. In the words of one Yukon summer missionary, "They are potential outcasts of their own people and are not quite up to the standards of the white intellect. In other words, they are 'betwixt and between' — a condition of pitiful helplessness." Experience in the south should have warned northern missionaries of the weaknesses of the residential school plan.

The residential school system forced painful adjustments for all family members. While the children were still young, parents had to decide if they would be sent to boarding school. They knew that deciding in favour of school meant that the children might not return home until they graduated at age sixteen, unless the family lived close to the school. Parents often regretted their decision, and petitioned the authorities for the return of their children. To their dismay, their appeals went unheeded (except for cases of extreme family hardship), as the government and missionaries believed that continued attendance was almost always in the child's best interests.

The first residential schools in the north were in the Mackenzie River valley. A small Anglican boarding school opened at Hay River in 1902, followed by a larger Catholic facility at Fort Resolution. By the 1930s, four boarding schools drew native children from throughout the region, including Inuit youngsters from the Mackenzie delta. The programme was expensive, costing the federal government more than $45,000 in 1939-40 (many times more than the $1370 allocated for the four day schools). Even then, the use of missionaries as teachers and administrators kept costs far lower than they otherwise would have been.

Although schooling and medical assistance were similar in the two territories, conditions varied in one important respect: the Mackenzie River valley was covered by treaties. Treaty 8, signed in 1899, and Treaty 11, accepted in 1921, could hardly be called negotiated treaties, for terms were simply imposed on the natives to clear the way for anticipated economic development. Treaty 8 was hastily implemented during the Klondike gold rush in anticipation of further mining activity in the upper Mackenzie River district. Successful drilling operations by an Imperial Oil crew at Norman Wells in 1920 provided the impetus for the second Mackenzie River treaty. The treaty party quickly visited the various trading centres, explained the document and collected signatures. Chiefs received $32 for signing, with most natives getting the standard $12 allotment. There were promises of a $5 annuity (more for Chiefs and headmen) for the future. The natives signed, but the haste of the "negotiation" process and improprieties in the signing suggested that little actual consultation actually occurred. The package had been presented to the natives as a fait accompli, for they could not change the wording of the document. Why did the natives sign? Probably because the government's determination to proceed was obvious and there was nothing to gain by not signing. The process was not designed to meet native needs; rather, its central purpose was to show southern businesses that the entire Mackenzie River valley was open for development.

The establishment of treaties spurred the government to expand its Indian Agent network, providing basic relief and medical services for most treaty Indians. The amounts allocated for such assistance remained very small, however, limiting the significance of the government's gestures. Even the outbreak of a major flu epidemic in 1928 failed to produce an expansion of medical services. More difficult to rebuff, however, were demands from the natives (supported by the missionaries), that Indian trapping and trading rights be guaranteed. The influx of white trappers and resulting competition for game led to racial tensions as well as a depletion of game. Although local Indian Agents, like T.W. Harris, and missionaries, particularly Bishop G. Breyant, supported native claims that the district be reserved for Indian hunters, territorial officials rejected the appeals. As the demand for furs peaked, over-hunting threatened the resource base and hence the native livelihood. It also appeared that the promises of Treaties 8 and 11 had been little more than public posturing.

In truth, the federal government was not totally inactive, although its moves had only a marginal effect. Without consulting the natives, the territorial administration moved in September 1923, to establish three game preserves (Yellowknife, 70,000 sq. mi.; Slave River, 2,152 sq. mi.; and Peel, 3,300 sq. mi.). In these areas, only treaty Indians were permitted to hunt, a decision which had unfortunate consequences for non-treaty natives and Metis who also relied on wild game. The creation of the game preserves hardly addressed the more substantial problems of increased competition, and did little for those treaty natives without access to the reserves. Not until the 1930s, when increased gold mining drew more whites to the district, did the territorial and federal administrations actually protect native hunting rights. The establishment of the almost 70,000 sq. mi. Mackenzie reserve, coupled with new trapping legislation in 1938, guaranteed natives preferred access to game. The protection, typically, came after resources had been seriously depleted, at a time when the fur market had fallen off, and when most whites in the area had drifted off into other economic pursuits.

Throughout the sub-Arctic, the federal government encouraged natives to continue their harvesting operations. Although the Mackenzie River valley treaties afforded some modest protection, conditions in the Northwest Territories were little better than those in the Yukon. In the latter region, the government refused even the modest guarantees of game preserves, preferring to leave the area open for mineral development. In both territories, federal officials hesitated to guarantee native access to game, although the limited support for education and other "improvement" programmes indicated the administrators' wish to leave the natives as nomadic harvesters. Native needs were not to interfere with potential white plans, either in hunting or mining. It was but one example of how a colonial administration system — territories ruled by a distant bureaucracy — worked to the detriment of the people, particularly the natives, of the north.

The Realities of Colonial Government

A better illustration of the control exercised by Ottawa is provided by the administration of regional government. During the gold rush, the Yukon enjoyed a slow movement toward self-government. Although signs remained mixed, Yukoners believed the federal government would grant greater autonomy and that the territory would move steadily down the path toward provincial status. That proved not to be so. As people left and revenue declined, the federal government sought to reverse the trend toward autonomy, and cut back on territorial expenditures.

The federal government rationalized operations as the economy contracted. A number of civil servants were fired, and several territorial and federal jobs were amalgamated. Dawson City, only recently incorporated, lost its municipal charter. The territorial legal system was similarly emasculated, as the Yukon Territorial Court shrank from three justices to one. The federal government clearly wished to lessen its northern commitments and did so with considerable relish. The positions of Commissioner and Gold Commissioner were consolidated into a single post in 1920. This joint position disappeared in turn in 1932, when the duties were transferred to the Territorial Comptroller. The range of authority continued to narrow, as federal officials linked more and more jobs together.

G.A. Jeckell's administrative career symbolized the collapse of a meaningful civil service. By 1932 when as Comptroller he became the territory's chief executive officer, Jeckell also held the positions of Agent for Public Works, Income Tax Inspector, ex-officio Mayor of Dawson, and Chief Registrar of Land Titles. Until after World War II, Jeckell virtually held the reins of territorial power in his hands. Yet his authority was more apparent than real, for actual power rested in the Ottawa offices of the federal government. The retrenchment process was, as James Lotz once commented, "a withering away of the state in a way in which Marx never envisaged. One man wore many hats, and the Commissioner was a virtual dictator, ruling the Territory on behalf of the federal government."

Nonetheless, Yukon conditions represented an advance over constitutional arrangements in the Northwest Territories. The Territories suffered from a lack of geographic unity. The Northwest Territories represented Canada's leftovers, made up in part of the land remaining after the provinces of Alberta and Saskatchewan had been created in 1905 and Manitoba's boundary was pushed northward in 1912. The Arctic archipelago, ceded by Britain in 1880, rounded out the territory. Still, it was a politically separate jurisdiction, managed by a single administration, and, for better or worse, locked into a single destiny. It would be without a regional administrator, however, for those in charge would run the territory from Ottawa.

Lt. Col. Fred White, Comptroller of the RNWMP, was named Commissioner of the Northwest Territories in 1905. Residing in Ottawa and with little civil service support, White could do little more than respond to reports on the north which crossed his already cluttered

desk. The Department of Indians Affairs maintained
an even greater presence than did the distant territorial
administration. Minor improvements came in 1921
when, under Commissioner W.W. Cory (deputy
minister of the Department of the Interior), a four-man
council based in Ottawa assumed administrative
responsibility. More important, the council took the
modest step of opening a branch headquarters at Fort
Smith, the major entry point to the territory, and
appointing territorial agents at several points around
the region.

These administrative changes proved to be only
cosmetic. The Northwest Territories Council met
irregularly and paid little attention to its responsibilities. Government services, minimal though they were,
came through federal departments, particularly the
RNWMP and Indian Affairs. As in the past, the police
performed the bulk of the duties, from enforcing hunting and trading regulations to conducting the census.
On a higher administrative level, federal supervision
of northern affairs was centred in the Northwest Territories Branch of the Department of the Interior, which
was established in 1921 (and renamed the N.W.T. and
Yukon Branch in 1923). Although this bureaucratic
shuffling suggested a growing awareness of the country's distinctive northern responsibilities, it was not to
be so.

Many of the civil servants were the strongest advocates of northern development, aided by small but
vibrant voices of regional protest. George Jeckell, I.O.
Finnie, and Dr. Charles Camsell were but three of
many federal and territorial officials who used their
offices to encourage a more enlightened attitude to the
territories. At the same time, however, the still-born
constitutional development of both territories robbed

them of a popularly elected assembly, the most obvious outlet for political agitation. Local newspapers, particularly the *Dawson Daily News*, and the Yukon's one MP, did try to protect regional interests, but often to no avail.

The north's colonial status also begat a dependent, colonial mentality. Status in the white sectors of the north typically rested on occupation and political clout. The key positions — Commissioner/Comptroller, Treasurer, Police Officer — were all federal appointees, giving civil servants tremendous influence. As revenues from mineral production and game harvests declined, both territorial administrations came to rely heavily on federal grants. In 1910 in the Yukon, for example, federal grants made up 60 per cent of territorial revenue, although that figure declined steadily to around 35 per cent by 1937 as the government consolidated its operations. With the civil servants providing social leadership, with decisions of vital importance made by federal departments, and with the governments dependent on federal grants, the citizens of the Yukon and Northwest Territories were only too aware of their colonial status.

Emblematic of the colonial attitude was the cavalier fashion with which the federal departments discussed altering territorial boundaries. In 1928, rumours abounded of a plan to annex the northern third of the Yukon to the Northwest Territories for administrative convenience. Federal officer I.O. Finnie wrote at the time, "It would not greatly concern the people of the Yukon," an opinion that likely would not have been borne out had the discussions been made public. Although the decision to proceed received cabinet approval, the collapse of the Herschel Island economy a few years later eliminated the need for the change.

A more serious challenge to the political integrity of the territories came in 1937, when British Columbia Premier T. "Duff" Pattullo attempted to annex the Yukon Territory. Pattullo had earlier lived in the Yukon and linked his vision of provincial development with the take-over of the north's resources. The federal government, anxious to rid itself of a financial burden, greeted the proposal favourably. Yukoners rose to the challenge, resentful of the suggestion that the stronger southern province would simply swallow up their territory. Both federal and provincial officials dismissed such objections and proceeded with their plans. Ironically, a small publicly-funded Catholic school in Dawson City provided an insurmountable stumbling block. Although it was a seemingly minor matter, it raised the spectre of a national Catholic-Protestant rift over educational rights (British Columbia did not fund separate schools). Faced with such a potential controversy, the ever-cautious Prime Minister William Lyon Mackenzie King capitulated. To Pattullo's dismay and the Yukoners' delight, the proposal was allowed to die. The Yukon retained the right to exist, although not because federal or provincial politicians accepted the need for territorial integrity.

The colonial pattern remained intact, reinforced rather than removed by the years of economic decline and re-orientation. The value of the Yukon and Northwest Territories was still determined by their utility to the south, and when that value was not clearly evident the region was ignored. The period from the end of the gold rush to the commencement of World War II was such a time. There was, seemingly, no recognition in official circles of the unique social and economic communities in the north, or at least, no willingness to assist that society through what obviously would be a difficult evolution. With constitutional authority firmly entrenched in Ottawa, advocates of regional autonomy found few supporters. The north would have to wait until another national purpose could be found for the region.

5
Boom and Bust in the Arctic

The fluctuations of the north's "boom-and-bust" economic order are particularly evident in the high Arctic (north of the treeline). Here, in the period up to World War II, separate booms based on whales and fur stimulated rapid growth and subsequent decline. The expansion and contraction altered Inuit life and depleted resources as it brought the imperatives of a southern market to bear on this sparsely populated area.

The Whaling Boom

Whales attracted the first wave of southern harvesters. Although the harsh, unforgiving climate posed a threat to the mariners, potential financial rewards brought them north by the score. The ponderous, ungainly Arctic whales fetched high prices in the right market. In these pre-petroleum days, whale blubber was used as oil for lamps and as a lubricant. More important were the massive chunks of baleen (whale-bone) taken from each mammal and used for a variety of products, including buggy whips and corset stays, that required both strength and flexibility. Early explorers noted large whale pods in Arctic waters, and a number of whalers headed northward into the commercially virgin waters.

The expansion proceeded slowly, impeded by the uncertainties of northern navigation, the imprecise maps of the high Arctic, the abundance of whales in more accessible waters, and the slow evolution of harvesting technology to suit northern conditions. As early as the 1720s, however, American whalers had entered Davis Strait. These first whalers kept to the sea, wary of the shore-bound ice pack. As activity expanded along Baffin Island, Cumberland Sound became, by the 1840s, the focal point for the new northern industry. Bountiful stocks and the availability of local Inuit labour combined to offer prime hunting conditions. Americans followed explorers into Lancaster Sound even before the Cumberland centre developed and, by the 1860s, pushed into Hudson Bay. With this last expansion, whalers had penetrated most of the productive districts in the eastern Arctic. Newly opened areas could not sustain hunting for long, however — the comparative immobility of the whales and relentless exploitation of the resource by the southern whalers ensured a rapid depletion of harvestable supplies.

The tale was replayed in brief in the western Arctic, where the dangerous task of navigating around the Alaskan peninsula severely restricted maritime activity. American whalers first pushed east of Bering Strait in 1848, but another forty years passed before Joe Tuckfield, travelling in an open whaleboat, reached Herschel Island from the west. His enthusiastic report of whaling prospects found a ready audience, and by the next fall whaling ships reached the island. Bountiful early returns — the *Grampus*, one of two ships sent in 1890-91, returned with over half a million dollars in cargo — stimulated a rapid expansion. Whale stocks around Herschel Island plummeted, forcing whalers to head further east. Within a decade, ships regularly crossed the mouth of the Mackenzie River and hunted off Baillie and Pullen Islands. Although it started later than did whaling in the east, the western Arctic whaling industry made up in intensity for what it lacked in longevity.

European whaling in the Arctic spanned many decades, from the early eighteenth to the early twentieth centuries, and underwent several major technological changes. Whaling posed impressive challenges, for capturing these long (up to 55 feet) and weighty animals was far from easy. Standard procedure involved launching several whaleboats — themselves solid craft — from the main ship. The pursuit boats approached the quarry, a harpoon was thrown, and a dangerous tug-of-war ensued, ending either when the whale tired and had been killed or when the harpoon-line broke. The season of open water whaling was considerably shorter in the north than in other districts, so adaptations were necessary. In the spring, while the main vessel remained locked in ice, whaleboats were hauled to the edge of open water and launched. Sleds, often manned by Inuit, were used to carry supplies to the boats and return the harvest to the factory ship. Developments in harpoon technology, like assistance in the delivery of the lance, or an explosive head triggered to explode on impact eased the process somewhat, but the killing of whales remained an arduous and dangerous task.

Whaling was, of course, hardly new to the Inuit and most whalers wisely capitalized on their well-honed skills. Native men worked on the whaleboats, ran sleds, and provided food, the latter being a particularly crucial function once the whalers began to winter in the north. The Inuit found a niche at virtually every point in the harvesting process, from the killing of the whales to making and mending suitable Arctic clothing. The whaling economic system was not unlike the fur trade in its dependence on native labour, although non-natives obviously played a far greater role in the actual killing process. The Inuit greeted the expansion of whaling much as the Indians to the south welcomed the fur traders. From Hudson Bay to Herschel Island, Inuit groups reoriented their seasonal activities to incorporate whaling and ensure regular contact with the ships.

The whalers brought a great deal that was attractive to the Inuit. Because the fur traders had not yet pushed this far northward, the Inuit lacked direct access to a supply of manufactured goods. Ship's captains, needing the Inuit as labourers or food gatherers, brought a supply of tools, guns, and other such items. Metal implements, particularly pots, long-bladed snow knives, guns, telescopes, and whaleboats all improved Inuit harvesting capacity, while luxury items, like southern foods and musical instruments, also found favour with the natives. The need for fresh food at Herschel Island, for example, encouraged the whalers to trade southern supplies for meat. The Inuit accepted the exchange, finding the processed foods and heavily sugared items quite palatable; they did not, unfortunately, recognize soon enough the impact of this radical change of diet on their health, especially dental health.

Although whaler-Inuit contact retained its co-operative nature, the ledger was never adequately balanced, for whaling was an extremely exploitative industry. Area after area was abandoned after the whaling resources were depleted; the whalers simply moved on to a new, hopefully profitable field. This recurring cycle of resource discovery, intensive harvesting and abandonment brought temporary prosperity to regional groups, but just as systematically induced resource depletion and economic dislocation. The vaunted Inuit mobility stood them in good stead for a time, as they followed the white whaling "settlements" along the coast. The chase — both of whales and whaling ships — was doomed to be a finite one.

The diseases wreaked even more havoc. As happened to the Indians of the sub-Arctic, the arrival of the white men unleashed a series of destructive epidemics which killed hundreds of Inuit. The structure of the whaling industry helped spread the diseases. Inuit gathered in semi-permanent villages near the whaling grounds, allowing for extended contact with the crewmen. The mariners unwittingly passed on diseases they carried from the south. Inuit mobility now became an enemy. After an outbreak, many fled for safer havens. They now became carriers, exposing other isolated bands to the alien and deadly germs. Imprecise population data for the Inuit and inconsistent reporting of the diseases by the whalers make it difficult to gauge the impact of the illnesses. Most likely, they were as destructive as the epidemics which swept through Indian populations.

Similarities across the Arctic in whaler-Inuit relations have established stereotypes: whalers plying the natives with liquor, Inuit ravaged by disease, and a shocking depletion of resources are the most common themes. These images derive predominantly from the experience in the western Arctic. The more controlled development of the eastern Arctic islands and Hudson Bay regions meant that relations there did not develop in such stark relief.

Perhaps because the development of whaling in the east proceeded more moderately, British and Canadian authorities were slow to assert their sovereignty in the area. The expansion of whaling carried notable, although not readily obvious, political implications.

By the mid-nineteenth century, Americans dominated the industry. Sovereignty over the Arctic islands had never been clearly established, and the creation of whaling settlements challenged the British assumption (based on the rights of discovery), that the territory belonged to them. In 1880, the British government transferred the Arctic islands to Canada, leaving the matter of asserting and enforcing ownership to the young Dominion. In the end, the region was saved for Canada, although largely by default, as Americans and other nationals who had established claims of their own through short-term occupation did not press their advantage.

Federal authorities were reluctant to pick up the challenge. Not until the turn of the century, when American and Norwegian explorers registered claims to portions of the Arctic archipelago and when diplomatic tensions raised fears in Canada about possible American expansion, did the government take much notice of the region. In 1903, the *Neptune* carried a joint NWMP-Geological Survey of Canada team into the region to investigate conditions and assert Canadian sovereignty. Further flag-waving ventures, mostly ship patrols, followed. The Canadians approached their declaration of ownership with typical paternalism, thinking the Inuit intellectually incapable of comprehending their real message. Historian W. Gillies Ross offers a description of the laughable declaration of Canadian sovereignty:

Here were a people [the Inuit] who had maintained intimate ties with foreign whalers for more than forty years being treated as simple, helpless, credulous savages. Here were men who possessed whaleboats, darting guns, shoulder guns, and all the sophisticated paraphernalia employed in the pursuit of bowhead whales, who hunted with telescopes and powerful repeating rifles, and who normally wore American trousers, shirts, jackets, hats and sunglasses. Here were women who used manufactured domestic implements and containers, who made up clothes on sewing machines, who attended shipboard dances in imported dresses, and who bore children sired by whalemen. To these people an officious, uniformed stranger [Inspector Moodie of the N.W.M.P.] was distributing underwear as if it were a priceless treasure and lecturing them on morals and their allegiance to a big white chief. When Moodie suggested that the Eskimos might wish to travel 500 miles to Churchill to send joyful messages of thanks to the King, no one responded.

Captain J.E. Bernier led several expeditions after the turn of the century to lay formal claim to the Arctic islands and to impose a modest level of control over economic activities in the region. As evidence of overhunting and the extent of non-Canadian harvesting came to light, new whaling regulations were issued. It was, typically, too late, as irreparable damage had already been done. The whaling period had been very profitable for southern business, sustained for over a century by the bountiful resources of the eastern Arctic. There was little positive benefit for the region beyond the introduction of new technology to the Inuit. Sadly, conditions to the west were even worse.

Herschel Island

Herschel Island was a most unlikely setting for a nineteenth-century Sodom and Gomorrah. The island, a small, unspectacular bit of land marked only by a fine natural harbour, sits a few miles off the Yukon's northern coast. Ships heading for the Beaufort Sea whaling grounds had to circle the Alaskan peninsula and coast through the dangerous waters along the north edge of the continent. Herschel Island was the first, and almost the only, sanctuary. Smaller wintering ports eventually developed further east, but only Herschel Island had a large enough harbour to contain the early fleet, when as many as fifteen ships would tie up in the cove.

It required more than a large number of whaling ships to create what anthropologist Diamond Jenness referred to as a "hive of debauchery." Crews in the eastern Arctic were noted for their comparative stability, and good captains could count on a number of men returning for several voyages. Herschel Island crews lacked that professionalism. Whaling firms, often unable to hire enough men legitimately, found other methods. Tavern keepers were paid to single out drunks who would be shanghaied or coerced into signing aboard an Arctic-bound whaler. Men who had been literally dragged on board often found, after a two-or three-year stint in the north that deductions had eaten up virtually their entire pay.

For the Herschel Island elite, meanwhile, life was not so unpleasant. Captains sometimes brought their wives north and the winter season witnessed a constant round of dinners, tea-parties and soirées. Given the conditions of their employment and the contrast in lifestyles, crewmen not surprisingly turned unruly on occasion.

Captains attempted to contain the anger by allowing the whalers free access to native camps and by making liquor widely available. Unlike in the east, where alcohol use was more closely regulated, on Herschel Island the booze flowed freely whenever the whaling ships arrived. Barrels of liquor were uncorked, and the crewmen and Inuit partied into an alcoholic stupor. Sailors and native women were paired off and clambered aboard ship. The debauchery scandalized missionaries and government officials who learned of the Herschel happenings, but the distant island seemed beyond the scope of spiritual or legal protection.

Anarchy appeared endemic, limited only by the tenuous authority of the ships' captains. But the captains were not particularly concerned about the unruly and destructive behaviour of their crews. Few expressed any special interest in the obvious problems facing the Inuit: debauchery, disease, over-hunting of much-needed local resources, and technological displacement. The decline of local Inuit influence, based only tenuously on the whalers' need for their skills in the first place, was exacerbated by the importation of Alaskan Inuit as caribou hunters. (The coastal Inuit were sea harvesters and lacked the specific skills for large-scale inland hunts). The cumulative effects of economic dislocations compounded by disease, led to the virtual disappearance of the indigenous population. By the 1920s, almost three-quarters of the remaining Inuit in the western Arctic were American migrants.

The official response to the destruction was modest, slow and too late. The Anglican church arrived first. The young missionary (and later Bishop of the Yukon), Isaac O. Stringer, reached Herschel Island in 1894, although he did not open a permanent mission for another three years. Even then, Stringer's inability to communicate effectively with the Inuit and his friendship with the whaling captains restricted his contribution to the issuance of petitions and pious pronouncements on the liquor trade. By the time Stringer established himself on the island, moreover, the whaling industry's decline was evident, and the days of debauchery more a memory than a regular event.

The Canadian government lagged behind. It was only when missionary and temperance groups picked up the chorus of protest that modest measures were taken. Even then, a laissez-faire attitude toward the inevitable dislocations of frontier development restricted official action. Herschel Island assumed greater importance, however, in the wake of the Canadian embarrassment over the Alaska boundary dispute. Still smarting from the diplomatic rebuke that saw a joint British, Canadian, and American panel decide in favour of the United States' position on the boundary, the Canadian government prepared to prevent further set-backs at American hands. The apparent American occupation of Herschel Island suddenly represented such a threat.

The plan was to show the flag and assert Canadian sovereignty; imposing federal law or extending federal services to this distant district held much lower priority. Sergeant F.J. Fitzgerald of the NWMP arrived in 1903 to establish a police post. The police, always prepared to disbelieve missionary accounts, found few signs of lawlessness and anarchy. Captains proved most co-operative, publicly echoing the southern concerns over debauchery and licentious behaviour. They obviously found the police of considerable assistance in their most difficult task, controlling their crews. Fitzgerald had, however, arrived too late, for the western Arctic whaling industry was already on the decline. In the days when the exploitation of the large Beaufort herds brought great wealth, the whalers might easily have resisted the imposition of Canadian laws and customs duties. It was much easier to be agreeable now that the trade had fallen off. Besides, any captain wishing to avoid the duties or remain beyond the sight of the law could simply bypass the Herschel Island supply depot. Canadian authorities took pride in their "effective" response to yet another "Yankee" incursion. That their intervention came too late to help the Inuit did not seem of much concern to them.

Nor was the government distressed by the obvious devastation of Arctic whale stocks. In the eastern Arctic, the long-established industry slowly chipped away at the resource base. According to statistics compiled by W. Gillies Ross, over 750 ships came north in the decade 1820-1830, capturing more than 8,000 whales. In contrast, between 1890 and 1900, only fifty-eight ships ventured into the area, returning with just 140 whales. By the turn of the century, the few whalers still coming north worked very hard for their modest gains. The previous whalers had been distressingly thorough, for by the time market forces undercut the industry in the early twentieth century, the whale herds had all but disappeared in the east.

In terms of stocks, the later development in the west offset the more efficient exploitation made possible by steam whaling. When synthetic products replaced baleen, and petroleum supplanted whale oil, the demand for whale by-products collapsed. After taking more than $13 million in whale products from the western Arctic between 1890 and 1907, whaling activity sputtered to a halt.

The whaling boom was over. Camps in the eastern Arctic lay abandoned. Herschel Island, now a small government outpost for the western Arctic, showed few signs of its boisterous past. The Inuit, having altered their seasonal habitation patterns, consumption patterns, and social activities to involve the whalers, found themselves suddenly abandoned, their skills no longer marketable, and the animal resources they depended on for survival, all but extinct in some areas.

The Arctic Fur Trade

The effects of the collapse of whaling were offset in part by the emergence of an Arctic fur trade. Inuit had traded furs with the whalers even in the early days of the whale hunt. What started as a minor side-line soon became an integral part of the whaling industry. Ships' captains wished to maintain friendly relations with the Inuit, and did so in part by carrying extensive stores of southern manufactured goods, some of which they traded for furs. The exchange soon gained a more regular footing, as the whalers discovered the handsome profits and open markets for the furs in southern ports. The fierce competition among whalers carried over into the fur trade, raising the prices paid to Inuit hunters accordingly.

Because the fur exchange was tangential to their main goal, the whalers ignored the standard conventions of the northern fur trade. The federal government had barred the sale of both alcohol and repeating rifles to the natives, the first to protect the natives from the consumption of the "evil" spirits, and the second to prevent over-hunting. The furs themselves, from the exotic musk-ox and polar bear to the highly valued white fox, generated tremendous interest in southern markets. Few fur companies, however, dared challenge the whalers' ascendancy in either the eastern or western Arctic. When the whaling ships stopped their regular voyages, however, they left an economic vacuum other firms were suddenly eager to fill.

The HBC led the fur trade expansion into the Arctic. The firm had two posts along the northern coast of

Hudson Bay by 1911, and the following year established a small outpost in the western Arctic. The trade did not become another monopoly situation, for each year several "floating" posts — trading ships — also vied for the Inuit's furs. The Arctic trading frontier unfolded cautiously, for the personal risk and high cost of Arctic trading did not justify daring commercial thrusts into the still little-known territories. The modest expansion solved the crisis of the Inuit insofar as it provided continued access to southern trade goods, but it did not signal a return to the economic prosperity of the whaling era.

The fur trade of the 1910s and 1920s did, however, reveal some significant departures from trade patterns further south. Numerous commentators — traders, missionaries and police officers — noted that the Inuit approached commercial opportunities in a different fashion from other natives. Unlike the Indians of the sub-Arctic, who had finite demands and limited acquisitive tendencies, the Inuit seemed most interested in property accumulation. Their demands and needs fell short of the capitalistic fervor of the whalers or traders, but they did stock-pile goods, pay their debts on time, and express unusual interest in luxury items. The Inuit were not unintelligent savages awed by southern baubles; instead, they recognized good commercial prospects, found much of the technology useful, and saw value in the private accumulation of wealth. F.H. Kitto recorded the extent of this materialism:

> No longer are they ignorant savages dwelling in igloos in winter and forced to eke out a pitiful existence in a terrific struggle against all the forces of nature. The igloos have given place to comfortable winter dwell-

ings of logs or rough lumber, in many cases finished with wall-board and dressed lumber.

White flour, sugar, butter, jam and canned food and other luxuries are included now in the diet. Long evenings are passed pleasantly listening to good music provided by expensive gramophones and radio sets. Brass and iron spring beds take the place of the only family couch of skins. Up-to-date sewing machines make the lot of women easier....Cameras, watches, thermos bottles, safety razors, high-powered rifles, and many other products of modern civilization are in general use.

It was a long way from the Inuit condition in the pre-contact period. There is little doubt that the Inuit welcomed and encouraged these economic changes.

The cycles of the Arctic exchange paralleled activities to the south. The same market forces which drew independent white traders and larger commercial operators into the sub-Arctic also brought them even further north. Fueled by an abnormal demand for white fox, returns escalated for both native and white participants in what quickly became the second Arctic boom. Following modest HBC moves, competitive traders expanded their activities. By the 1920s, traders criss-crossed the far north, creating a network which stretched from Herschel Island to Baffin Island. (Even areas previously deemed unfruitful by Europeans, like Coronation Gulf and Queen Maud Gulf, attracted their share of traders.)

Although the HBC made the first steps, the smaller operators forced the pace of expansion and maintained the competitive atmosphere. Independents, often trappers themselves, ignored trading conventions, and pushed steadily beyond the boundaries of the established trade. At the height of the trade, from 1925 to

1929, almost seventy posts operated at fifty-eight locations throughout the Arctic (there were an additional twenty-one posts in the Keewatin district). Buttressed by its impressive financial and organizational advantages, the HBC still dominated the industry, but several medium-sized companies challenged the established firm's monopolistic tendencies.

The depression of the 1930s dampened the demand for northern furs. The staple of the Arctic trade, the white fox, dropped to one-fifth of its peak value by mid-decade. Poorly financed independents and several of the larger firms were forced out of business. The trade did not collapse; more furs were trapped and traded as Inuit and whites attempted to maintain earlier high incomes. Many traders held on for a few years. But as the depression deepened, traders gathered in key locations, maintaining competition through proximity rather than by pushing back the trading frontier. The death knell of the fur boom was sounded in 1938, when the HBC bought out its principal competitor, the Canalaska Trading Company.

Herschel and Baillie Islands, both former wintering stops for the whalers, had served as supply bases for the western Arctic trade. As early as 1915, the HBC imported supplies by ship to Herschel Island, a pattern soon adopted by its competitors. The orderly nature of the commercial fur trade, at least when compared to the earlier whaling era, allowed the island to develop a settled air. With RNWMP officers and Anglican missionaries on site, the community became a model of propriety and sobriety. But as the fur trade declined, so did Herschel Island. In 1937, the HBC clerk noted laconically, "No fur this year, mostly cash sales." The trading post and police station soon closed down. Further contraction of the trade, particularly the concentration of HBC operations at Tuktoyaktuk, signaled the end of the Baillie camp as well. The dying communities told the story of the fur trade all too well.

The natives had, in some ways, benefited from the boom. Skilled Inuit trappers often calculated their returns in the thousands of dollars. Prices of trade goods were obviously higher than in the south due to transportation costs; even so, the Inuit income level often exceeded the average annual wages for many industrial workers. Much of the money was reinvested in hunting supplies. Several dozen of the wealthier Inuit purchased motorized ocean schooners, a sign of the obvious profitability of this twentieth-century commercial frontier. The pattern was not dissimilar to that of the whaling era, although the prosperity was now more widespread.

Such prosperity carried significant costs. In many parts of the central and eastern Arctic, native-white contact had been very limited before 1920. Thereafter, these Inuit were rapidly integrated into the fur trade economy and drawn away from patterns of self-sufficiency and group interdependence. New technology obviously aided harvesting, but not without damage to animal stocks and native cultural values. Increased interracial contact brought tensions and occasionally violent confrontations. The impact of these changes appeared in striking relief when the boom ended. Now cash-poor and with limited access to southern supplies, the Inuit often could not maintain the goods and equipment they had purchased. Rifles that could not be repaired were discarded. Schooners were beached and abandoned. The Inuit were being forced to move back toward their former self-sufficient lifestyle although, as historian Morris Zaslow pointed out, "tastes had changed and old skills had atrophied."

But in one important sense there was no turning back. The fur trade boom reinforced the importance of commercial exchange to the Inuit. Changes in settlement patterns and harvesting pursuits hereafter were designed to provide access to a trading post and a supply of manufactured goods.

The Federal Government and the Arctic

In its general features — rapid expansion, intense competition, and precipitous decline — the Arctic fur trade pattern was not unlike that of the whaling era. The surprising intervention of the federal government set the trapping frontier off from the earlier period. Perhaps the whalers' debauchery encouraged more action; perhaps the fact that missionaries, scientists, and police officers were in the north, able to identify an impending crisis, convinced the government to move. The HBC even encouraged federal regulation, although their submissions smacked of commercial self-interest. For a variety of reasons, the government responded. White commercial hunters were barred from the Arctic islands, the use of "floating" trading posts was prohibited, as was the practice of "tripping," or visiting the Inuit in their camps. By 1926, all the Arctic islands and the coastline east of Bathurst Inlet had been declared off-limits to non-native hunters. The trading regulations and changes to general hunting laws now gave federal authorities far greater control over the harvesting of game.

The main beneficiary of this government involvement was in fact the HBC. Indeed many of the new regulations were inspired by HBC suggestions. The situation was reminiscent of the role assigned the Canadian Pacific Railway during the early development of the western plains, when the railway company appeared to have the ear of the government, and regulations seemed to unduly favour the increasingly unpopular monopoly. In the north, independent traders were deemed (not incorrectly), to be concerned only with short-term gains, while the stolid HBC cast an aura of stability and permanence. This continuity, unfamiliar in a land characterized by frequent change, made the company a favoured corporate citizen.

The government's initiatives likely prevented the despoliation of resources which had marred the whaling frontier. The measures were, however, preventative, not positive steps to integrate the north and its inhabitants into some broader national framework. To most southern officials, the Arctic was too different, too isolated, too underdeveloped — in sum, all but irrelevant — and they could see little validity in extending medical, health, or educational programmes throughout this vast district. The federal response was to encourage Inuit self-sufficiency, much as the plan in the Yukon and Mackenzie River valleys was to leave the Indians as Indians. Ottawa expected the Inuit to remain as nomadic harvesters and saw the government's function as providing a measure of stability and control over an isolated region. The programme fit Inuit desires — although they were not consulted — but it was not founded on a humanitarian impulse. Leaving the Inuit alone, and preventing a few whites from undercutting the natives' economic position was simply a cost-effective means of administering Inuit affairs.

Legal and constitutional abnormalities prevented the easy extension of federal services to the Inuit. Although the government unofficially accepted its obligations to the Arctic dwellers, there was no formal requirement that federal aid be provided. Confusion reigned until the 1930s over which department was responsible for Inuit affairs. Although administered under the Indian Act of 1924, the Inuit were technically not covered by that legislation; they therefore retained full rights as Canadian citizens. After a lengthy and ludicrous debate over whether or not Inuit were Indians (and therefore under the Indian Act), the Supreme Court of Canada ruled, in 1939, that they were indeed Indians. Although questionable on anthropological grounds, the decision at least placed Inuit affairs on a more formal basis.

The government had not entirely ignored Inuit needs, although financial restraints ensured that any offerings were kept to a minimum. As in the sub-Arctic, federal authorities relied heavily on missionaries to provide schooling and hospital care. At Herschel Island, Isaac Stringer and his replacement, Charles Whittaker, offered occasional day school classes. The education effort was expanded in 1928 when the Department of the Interior authorized the construction of an Anglican residential school at Shingle Point, west of the Mackenzie River. The school was closed in 1935, as Bishop Archibald Fleming reorganized church activities in the western Arctic around the Mackenzie delta town of Aklavik. The Inuit followed the church's lead, attracted partly by the school and hospital, but drawn more by the muskrat flats of the delta which provided a welcome alternative to the now-depressed fox trade.

Similar arrangements were made for the eastern Arctic. Missionaries ran government-financed schools, sent Inuit children to residential schools further south, and offered modest welfare and medical assistance at their mission stations. The Anglican Church also led the missionaries north into the eastern Arctic, opening a hospital at Pagnirtung on Baffin Island in 1928.

Sovereignty and Law Enforcement

That Canada felt the need, well into the twentieth century, to demonstrate its sovereignty over the Arctic indicates the lack of attention granted to the northern latitudes. The same forces which compelled the government to send the NWMP to both Herschel Island and Hudson Bay in 1903 convinced them to continue their flag-waving. Captain Bernier's voyages in the *Arctic* (1909-1911) permitted the government to lay formal claim to the Arctic archipelago. On a more grandiose scale, the geographic and scientific investigations of the Canadian Arctic Expedition of 1913-1918 demonstrated the federal interest in claiming its northland.

These modest assertions of sovereignty, devoid of physical occupation, did not deter others from assuming that the Arctic remained to be claimed. Exploratory ventures by Norwegian Roald Amundsen, who, in a voyage between 1903 and 1906, became the first to navigate the northwest passage, and American Robert E. Peary, threatened Canada's tenuous ownership. Even more contentious were claims resulting from Otto Sverdrup's explorations of 1899-1903, during which he discovered a chain of islands — Axel Heiberg, Amund Rignes and Ellef Rignes (named after his brewery sponsors) in the western portion of the Arctic archipelago. Most of the explorations passed without comment from the Canadian government, but Sverdup's discoveries were followed by semi-official territorial claims on behalf of the Norwegian government. The assertion was half-hearted at best, and was settled by a payment of $67,000 to Sverdrup by the Canadian government in 1930. The establishment of the Artic Island Preserve in 1926 was designed to prevent any further such controversies by requiring all explorers or scientists to obtain official permits before entering the area.

The countries involved, particularly the United States, Norway, and Denmark, did not push their claims with much enthusiasm. For them as for Canada, the Arctic was a scientific curiosity, not a land worth occupying.

Several federal measures had ensured a more regular assertion of symbolic sovereignty. In 1922, the government renewed the Eastern Arctic patrol, sending a ship north each year. These trips allowed the government to show the flag, supply an expanding network of Royal Canadian Mounted Police posts and establish more regular contact with the Inuit. The police posts provided very tangible evidence of Canadian ownership. Several posts, like Dundas Harbour and Bache Peninsula, were there solely to establish sovereignty. Police officers at such centres had few, if any local duties, for there were no permanent local inhabitants. Other posts provided a range of government services from a post office to the sale of fishing licences, as well as ensuring the enforcement of Canadian law and order. The police expanded their presence by undertaking lengthy patrols.

The police also brought Canadian law to the Arctic; as in the sub-Arctic regions, they experienced few difficulties. The ease of implementation rested on the Inuit's ready acceptance of most Canadian laws and the flexible enforcement of them by the police. Breaches of game regulations and minor criminal matters were usually dealt with by personal explanation to the offender, at least for the first offence. The police recognized that imposing a foreign set of laws represented a major assault on native forms of social control and they modified their goals accordingly. As long as the Inuit respected the sanctity of private property and did not threaten white adventurers, they were treated benignly. As they had done in the south, the police gradually implemented the laws more strictly, until the Inuit lived under the full strength of federal supervision.

The transition from gentle respect for Inuit practice to forced adherence to Canadian laws was symbolized by the police's handling of a series of highly publicized murders in the 1910s and 1920s. Explorers H.V. Radford and George Street were murdered by Inuit hunters in 1912. The offenders were tracked down — the police always get their man in the north too — but, convinced the attack had been provoked, the police let the men off with a warning. The following year, two Oblate priests, Fathers Rouvière and Le Roux, were killed by two Inuit, Sinnisiak and Uluksuk. The government wanted to make an example of the murderers, but stopped short of imposing a death sentence. The two were imprisoned at Fort Resolution, officially for life, but they were pampered more than incarcerated and both were released after two years. Although the punishment was scarcely severe, enforcement of the law had advanced to a new phase.

The real test came in 1923, when two Inuit from the Coppermine River area, Alikomiak and Tatimagana, stood accused of several murders, including those of Corporal Doak of the RCMP and Otto Binder, an HBC trader. Because the attack appeared to have been unprovoked (and possibly because a police officer was killed), the government brought down the full weight of the law. In an unconventional (and not totally impartial) murder trial held at Herschel Island, the accused were found guilty. After a prolonged debate, the government decided in 1924 that the two men should be executed. They died at Herschel Island on 1 February 1924. While these dramatic events scarcely typified police work in the north, they did symbolize the gradual hardening in the application of Canadian law. The Inuit were slowly but firmly brought under the umbrella of federal enforcement, and once there, were expected to respect national laws.

The police themselves were symbols of the government's apparent commitment to the Arctic. Their patrolling and voluntary isolation in the formidable northern hinterland made for fine drama which reinforced existing images of Canada's police force. Saddled with responsibility for virtually all federal services, the police accepted their burden with few public complaints. With only a handful of men and a widely scattered network of posts, they could actually do little. A sea-going detachment, housed in the famous *St. Roch*, added to police resources when brought on line in 1928, but given the large territories its commanders were responsible for, the ship's main function was to continue the tradition of showing the flag.

Christian Missions to the Inuit

That the government acted at all was due, in part, to the constant appeals of northern missionaries, who had their own agenda for the Inuit. The Anglican missionary, Isaac Stringer and his wife remained at Herschel Island until 1901, when they were replaced by Charles Whittaker. A rather acerbic character, Charles Whittaker made few friends among the white population, but dedicated years of service to the Inuit. Catholic attempts to follow the Anglican lead fell short. The murder of Father Rouvière and Father Le Roux in 1912 stopped a planned Oblate expansion into the western and central Arctic in its tracks.

The pattern was similar in the east, with initial Anglican moves followed by a Catholic attempt to catch up. Contact was limited by the scattered population and difficulties in supplying the isolated missions. Anglican missionaries reached Baillie Island in the early 1900s, and in 1912 Father Turgetil of the Oblates opened a mission at Chesterfield Inlet in the Keewatin District. Arctic conditions prevented the denominations from blanketing the region as they had attempted to do in the sub-Arctic, although the inter-church rivalry remained strong and the evangelical impulse irrepressible. The missions were not restricted to spiritual lessons, for limited government aid allowed the provision of modest educational and health services.

It is difficult to gauge the effect on the natives of the Anglican and Catholic missions, particularly since contact tended to be sporadic. As had happened elsewhere when native and white spiritual beliefs met, several "prophet" movements arose, offering amalgamations of the new gospel and aboriginal beliefs. The movements flared only briefly, snuffed out by missionary opposition and limited support. As in the south, missionaries enjoyed little success until they mastered the language or recruited native lay readers. Real gains came slowly and irregularly, although interfaith competition sustained the well-established rush to baptize.

The most noticeable sign that Christianity had taken root emerged in the western Arctic in 1900. With all the elements of a classic "awakening," a wave of conversions swept along the coast from Herschel to Baillie Islands. Anglican missionaries, especially Charles Whittaker, saw the transformation as the culmination of a decade's hard work. Scientist-explorer V. Stefansson saw the episode more critically, writing it off as a passing fad. The mass conversion may be explained by population shifts, for many Christian Inuit, educated by Moravians in Alaska, had migrated eastward. They brought their faith and (unlike the white missionaries) made the gospel immediately relevant to other Inuit.

Missionary-Inuit contact was not without its accomplishments for the churches. By the 1930s, both Anglicans and Catholics could claim numerous baptisms, a growing list of Inuit lay readers, and, for the Anglicans, a few ordained ministers. Missionary restrictions on polygamy, native celebrations and other cultural activities were gradually observed, although with obvious damage to Inuit society. The clergy's desire to "civilize" the Inuit similarly persuaded them to send children to distant residential schools, at Aklavik for Anglicans and further south for Catholics. Inuit students faced years of separation from their parents and community and, after their time at the boarding school, found the readjustment to their former homes painful and difficult. The denominational disputes further divided communities, groups, and even families along religious lines. As always, then, the missionary legacy was mixed. The clergy's zeal and dedication remained laudable, but it was paternalism and general disapproval of Inuit society that encouraged them to pursue their plan for societal reform. At the other extreme, missionaries quickly became the principal white spokespeople for Inuit rights and performed yeoman service in representing Inuit demands (as anticipated and embellished by the clergy) to the federal government.

Vilhjalmur Stefansson and the Arctic

Missionaries were not the only outsiders to discover the Arctic and its inhabitants in the early twentieth century. A southern fascination with the Inuit gradually took on a scientific perspective. Scientists Edouard de Sainville and Frank Russell reached Herschel Island as early as 1894, drawn by the lack of knowledge about this unique region. Others followed. Roald Amundsen led his famous Gjoa Expedition in 1903-1906.

Through their own published reports and journalistic accounts of their exploits, these adventurers fueled a renewed interest in the high Arctic. But none promoted the north, or at least his vision of the north, as did Vilhjalmur Stefansson. This Canadian-born, Icelandic-American scientist first entered the region in 1906, when he found the reputed "blond eskimos" of Victoria Island. Stefansson had encountered the Copper Inuit during his travels, and made note of their "European" characteristics. The explorer thought they might be descendants of members of the lost Franklin expedition or perhaps of Norwegian colonists from Greenland. When journalists broadcast this apparent "discovery," Stefansson's credibility in the scientific community was seriously attacked.

Stefansson was not deterred. He returned north in 1908, travelling among the Inuit from the north slope of Alaska to the Coronation Gulf. Stefansson was a skilled promoter, enjoyed public lecturing, and held a particular vision of the future of the north. This vision included an idealized notion of the "Friendly Arctic," for Stefansson believed that a resourceful, capable person could easily live off the land. Moreover, he argued, western civilization was on a northward course, re-invigorated by its gradual, irrevocable climb toward northern latitudes.

It was a powerful message, made all the stronger by Stefansson's loyal following among the media and a faction in the scientific community. He seemed, on the surface, to be the consumate promoter of the Canadian north, idolized by a large public following in southern Canada and the United States, an anthropologist/scientist of international repute, and one of the last men to discover further islands in the Arctic archipelago (Brock, Borden and Meighen).

That respect was not duplicated in the north. Police officers, missionaries, and traders questioned his sense of the Arctic. Government agents feared people would buy the "Friendly Arctic" idea. They asked for regulations which would keep such naïve southerners out of the region. One of his co-explorers, K.G. Chipman, summarized the feelings of many northerners in 1915:

> I learn here [Herschel Island] that V.S. [Stefansson] completely succeeded in "getting the goat" of everybody here and at Fort McPherson. It is strange, but no one seems to have a good word for him. Seldom have I seen a man for whom there were fewer good words than is the case with V.S. along the coast.

Stefansson and the police squared off repeatedly over the years about the best means of Arctic travel, and he was sharply critical of Anglican missionary work. The regional opposition meant little to Stefansson, for, as a self-styled man of vision, he foresaw a much better future for the northland than that presided over by a few petty policemen and missionaries. Stefansson went on extended speaking tours after each trip north, raising money for further expeditions and trying to generate a ground-swell of support among government officials and businessmen for his Arctic dream.

In 1913, in the midst of planning his largest expedition ever, Stefansson approached the Canadian government. Stefansson's requests for financial assistance, backed by the Geological Survey of Canada, were accepted and the Canadian Arctic Expedition of 1913-1918 was launched. The federal involvement altered the original plan, for the expanded exploration team included a number of researchers assigned to specific investigations. Stefansson, still planning the bold thrust which would forever etch his name in the annals of Arctic exploration, wanted a more nomadic, free-form mission. The apparent conflict was partially remedied by splitting the force in two. R.M. Anderson led the southern party, which conducted experiments along the Arctic coast, while Stefansson led the northern branch to search for the "blond" Inuit and to chart unknown districts in the Arctic archipelago.

The expedition foundered from the beginning, a monument to Stefansson's misplaced enthusiasm and hasty preparations. The *Karluk*, bearing Stefansson and most of the supplies for the northern party, became trapped in ice and eventually sank. Before a rescue could be effected, sixteen of the twenty-eight crew members aboard died. Stefansson, who had left the ship before the catastrophe, continued on. To do so, he claimed supplies allocated for Anderson's team, a move which increased tensions between the flamboyant American and the research-oriented Canadian scientist.

The southern expedition branch, made up of survey-ors, geologists, anthropologists, and natural scientists, worked along the coast until it was recalled in 1916. Stefansson travelled further north, discovering several previously unknown islands, and visiting with the Inuit. Yet his real work began when he left the area in 1918. While the other scientists summarized their findings and circulated their work through the small Canadian academic community, Stefansson went public. Through a well-promoted lecture series and the release of his book, *The Friendly Arctic*, he attempted to give legit-imacy to his notion of an easily developed northland. With the Klondike gold rush now a fading memory, southern audiences seemed ready for such a message. Although not interested in going north themselves, many citizens supported Stefansson and pressured the Canadian government and southern business to take up the explorer's challenge.

But Stefansson's further attempts to gain federal government backing failed. His insistence that Canada press its tenuous claim to Wrangel Island seriously damaged his credibility. In addition, the criticisms that Stefansson continued to level at fellow scientists, police officers, and missionaries began to rebound.

Undaunted, Stefansson began promoting his idea of herding reindeer. His enthusiasm pushed a pilot project through, and even secured the backing of the HBC. But by 1925 the operation was moribund, for the simple reason that the Baffin Island site chosen for the first herd could not not support the animals.

Stefansson's influence waned by the mid-1920s. The fracas over Wrangel Island, (which included a disas-trous attempt sponsored by Stefansson to colonize the island), the reindeer project, and numerous scientific controversies undermined his academic stature. The opinion expressed earlier by northerners appeared to be correct; Stefansson was a headstrong idealist, unforgiving of those who opposed or criticized his views. That he enjoyed so much fame perhaps further indicates the lack of awareness of northern realities and a continued susceptibility in the south to fantastic images of the northern frontier.

Stefansson's expeditions, particularly the Canadian Arctic Expedition, did contribute to a growing scientific interest in the Arctic, one that quickly outgrew the promoter. Physical and natural scientists came north in increasing numbers (although little support was available from Ottawa). Stefansson had also reawakened public interest in the Inuit. Diamond Jenness — one of Canada's most honoured anthropologists — first came north with the southern party of the Canadian Arctic Expedition and commenced an association that would last a lifetime. The federal government instituted its permit programme for northern field trips and imposed strict rules on the export of cultural artifacts, to keep the often acquisitive scientific and pseudo-scientific expeditions from getting out of control. Numerous anthropologists came in subsequent years to study the Inuit. Government and university scientists established research stations to study the weather, animal life, and Arctic geology. Always a curiosity, the Arctic became a human and physical laboratory. Numerous reports, although often hidden in obscure scholastic tomes, provided business and government with vastly improved information on northern conditions and allowed for much more realistic planning than had Stefansson's idealistic notions.

Before World War II, the Canadian government and people clearly had little interest in the northern reaches of their colonies. There was a certain fascination with the enormous size of this area, and a special pride in the massive presence of Canada on maps of the world. But this interest extended little beyond moves to keep the Arctic Canadian and prevent the despoliation of remaining resources.

A colonial pattern had been set. Plans to integrate the Arctic into a broader development scheme simply did not exist. Business and government instead responded to new resource discoveries with little foresight. The wild fluctuations in growth, which southerners wrote off as a "natural" part of the northern economy, had had severe effects on both resources and inhabitants. To government officials, however, there appeared to be few options, for their southern viewpoint blurred their perspective. There was little direct concern for the Inuit and the few white residents, and regional needs were repeatedly subordinated to a national preoccupation with limiting expenditures and keeping other countries at bay until another use could be found for the Arctic.

6
The Army's North

During the First World War, northern Canadians had struggled to demonstrate their interest in the confrontation raging on the distant battlefields of Europe. When war flared again on the international stage, the north found itself swept along, not on the front lines, but as a seemingly vital part of the plans for the defence of North America. Eyes turned slowly to the far northwest as the United States and Canada prepared for a Japanese assault. The attack never came — indeed, it was never a realistic threat — but the wartime emergency rekindled southern interest in the north and started a dramatic transformation of the Yukon and Northwest Territories.

Northerners felt the impact of the war only gradually. Increased demand for minerals in war materials production stimulated exploration and development, but the transition from the comparative inactivity of the late 1930s proceeded slowly. Numerous enlistments in the Canadian forces and sizable donations to patriotic societies illustrated the continuing effort to parade national allegiance, but these northern contributions elicited little interest on the national stage.

In the war's early phases, certain public angst over the possibility of a Japanese attack on Canada's west coast was not shared by military planners. That complacency disappeared on 7 December 1941, the day of the blistering Japanese attack on Pearl Harbour.

Military planners now focused their attentions on northern British Columbia, the Yukon, and Alaska: naval and air defences along the coast were shored up, but many were unsure of how to prepare for a land-based invasion. Such concerns gained even more urgency when, in June 1942, Japanese forces landed in the Aleutian Islands. The invasion was a minor one, repulsed through joint Canadian-American action, but public fear of a Japanese invasion swelled.

The north was not defenceless, for its protection was as much geographic as military. Air transport officials in Ottawa believed that the Great Circle Route from Canada to China would shortly become a major commercial airway, and work had started before the war on a series of airfields connecting Edmonton, Alberta and Fairbanks, Alaska.

The Building of the Alaska Highway

Air transport, although valuable, scarcely constituted a reasonable defence strategy. Acting in advance of Canadian military authorities, American planners began consideration of a road to Alaska. The idea was as old as the Klondike gold rush, but now gained new urgency.

With the support of British Columbia Premier Simon Tolmie, the United States government in 1930 appointed a commission of six (including three Canadians) to study the feasability of such a road. The project stalled, partially because Canadians saw the economic benefits of a highway to Alaska flowing disproportionately to the United States. More important, governments in the depression years were not prepared to risk much money on such monumental undertakings.

The highway to Alaska found a new promoter in Tolmie's successor, T. "Duff" Pattullo, who was elected in 1933. Pattullo's northern experience convinced him of the untapped potential of the province's frontier districts. Pattullo found ready support among American politicians. He could not, however, overcome the caution of Prime Minister William Lyon Mackenzie King. A fiscal conservative with little interest in the country's north, King saw only cost, not benefit, in Pattullo's dreams. When the B.C. premier attempted to bypass the federal government by appealing directly to the United States, King was livid. The Prime Minister agreed to a Canadian Alaska Highway Commission to parallel a similar American study, then ensured that the Canadian team had little opportunity to complete its work. (Charles Stewart, seriously ill in hospital at the time, was appointed commission chairman, and was unable to start work for six months). The Prime Minister's attempts to scuttle Pattullo's grandiose and expensive vision worked. By 1940, the proposal died and Pattullo's northern dream faded.

The Canadian and American commissions did serve one useful function. When the project resurfaced in 1942 under urgent wartime conditions, planners could draw on a sizable body of financial and engineering data. The principal issue to be decided was the route. The three main options included a coastal route, running north from Hazelton, B.C. to Whitehorse; a central route, linking Prince George and Dawson City; and a prairie route, following the air route from Edmonton to Fairbanks. Each option had attractions and liabilities, according to the criteria of vulnerability to enemy attack, ease of construction, access to resources and usefulness to existing settlements. Wartime was not the occasion for prolonged study, however, and American military planners pressed for a speedy decision.

On the surface, the questions at hand were obvious: which route; when does construction begin; and who will pay? In fact, the real issue was whether or not the highway was even required. With air and sea lanes open, there was actually little need to build new lines of communication and supply to Alaska. When American proposals for a highway emerged before December 1941, military authorities were quick to condemn the idea. The Japanese attack altered the equation. Politicians and armchair strategists throughout the civil service called for the immediate resurrection of highway plans, but military planners were less enthusiastic. Colonel A.R. Wilson of the War Department wrote: "The amount of work to be undertaken at the present time or in the immediate future depends upon a careful evaluation of the amount of machinery, material, engineering talent, labour and funds which can be diverted from other national defense projects which may be more important." The supply needs of Alaska, military officials claimed, could be met through existing means. Without having consulted the navy, hitherto responsible for supplying the northern territory, and with a negative report from military strategists in hand, the U.S. government nonetheless decided to proceed with construction.

Canadian military officials offered a similarly negative assessment, and Ottawa agreed that the country would not undertake the project. But now, in February 1942, the American government was pushing the highway and offering to pay the costs. H. L. Keenleyside, Assistant Under-Secretary of State for External Affairs, stated bluntly:

> The United States Government is now so insistent...that the Canadian government cannot possibly

allow itself to be put into the position of barring...land access to Alaska...[T]his agreement should be recognized, in our own minds at least, as being based on political and not on strategic grounds. The political argument, given the attitude of Washington, is inescapable; the strategic argument, in my opinion, is a most dubious egg.

Canada could not stand in the Americans' way. And why should it? The U.S. proposed to pay for a highway through previously inaccessible Canadian territory. If Americans wanted to spend millions of dollars on a road of questionable utility, and if they wished to "borrow" the Canadian northwest for the duration of the war to accomplish the task, the Canadian government saw no reason to oppose the project. So, on 5 March 1942, official Canadian permission was granted.

American officials perhaps believed that the Pacific fleet could not quickly recover from the debacle at Pearl Harbour, and could not bring themselves to rely on shipping as the only line of supply to Alaska. Still, Alaska was obviously of low priority to the Japanese, and American military resources were desperately required in other theatres of war. It is as yet unclear why United States politicians and civil servants overruled their military advisors. If the highway was not needed for defence, the rationale may have been its tremendous psychological and propaganda value to a continent caught in the first dark years of the second world war. Perhaps to reassure a doubting and fearful North American population, the building of the highway to Alaska "proved" that preparations were underway for continental defence.

With the go-ahead received, the first priority was to select a route. The Americans had long supported the coastal route, largely because it provided access to the scattered settlements of the Alaskan panhandle. B.C. politicians, notably Pattullo, favoured the central route, as it promised to open up vast tracts of mineralized lands. In the end, military planners rejected both suggestions. The U.S. Corps of Engineers opted for the prairie route. This decision reflected urgent military needs, not Canada's economic requirements, a fact that became obvious at war's end.

Although several Canadian surveyors had been busy locating airports and laying out connecting roads before the war, there was little precise information available. The responsibility for selecting the exact course fell to project manager Colonel William Hoge of the U.S. Corps of Engineers. Aerial photography, then in its infancy, greatly assisted Hoge's efforts. Even then, the plan was hardly that of a well-sited civilian highway. The operative concern was speed; the engineers were instructed to leave upgrading for a later date.

Hoge faced a monumental challenge. He had 11,000 workers at his disposal and was expected to push a rough highway through to Fairbanks before 1942 was out. The engineering regiments were broken into fourteen branches, each responsible for a particular section of the highway. Work proceeded systematically both north and south from several supply points on the route, ensuring rapid completion.

The U.S. Army did not tackle the actual construction of the highway itself. Rather, its task was to survey and construct a "pioneer" road. The Public Roads Administration (a U.S. civilian agency) would upgrade the road to appropriate civilian standards. Hoge, O'Connor, and the army attacked their job with classic American military resolve. Cost seemed of little concern, a fact noted by local residents who witnessed the inefficient use of equipment and supplies. Although speed was essential, logistical "snafus" were inevitable. One regiment north of Whitehorse began work with hand tools as they waited for their heavy equipment to arrive. The White Pass and Yukon Route Railway, taken over for the duration of the war, worked at peak capacity to funnel trainloads of supplies to the construction teams. Meanwhile, the workers, many of them American blacks, pushed on through unfamiliar territory in a harsh climate. They cursed the mosquitoes, the long summer days which lengthened their hours of work, and the muskeg which bogged down their equipment. The American soldiers were particularly ill-prepared for the winter, often lacking proper clothing and an awareness of the dangers of prolonged exposure to sub-zero temperatures.

The work on this pioneer road was rudimentary at best. Hastily-built bridges collapsed during rain storms or under the strain of heavy loads. Few improvements were made to the road surface; that task awaited the civilian contractors already on their way north. The challenge of muskeg was met by laying a corduroy (log) surface or by stripping away the upper covering and building on the firmer soil underneath. This latter process created a more serious problem: stripping uncovered a layer of permafrost, which quickly turned to a quagmire once exposed to the warming air. Crews repeatedly built over permafrost areas, only to have the roadbed disappear in a sea of mud.

Machines against permafrost, men against the northern elements — it all made for great drama. Not since the Klondike gold rush had the north known such fame. Radio programmes and newspaper articles, their accounts couched in a suitably mystifying cloud of secrecy, told people in the south of the progress of this great military venture. While Allied efforts else-where enjoyed few successes, North Americans could note with some satisfaction that the battle to defend the northwest was being won. On 20 November 1942, at a place called Soldier's Summit near Kluane Lake, the Alaska Highway was officially opened. The army had done its job; the pioneer road had been opened on schedule.

The first year's work did not finish the task, although little attention has been given to the workers and engineers who followed the army north. Even as the U.S. Army started its work, the Public Roads Administration began mobilizing its teams. Although the army retained final authority, the PRA was to convert the rough pioneer road into a finished gravel highway. In the original Canada-United States highway agreement, the Americans undertook to construct a 36-foot-wide (later reduced to 25 feet) all-weather road.

The Public Roads Administration co-ordinated the project, providing engineering and administrative services, but contracted out the actual construction work to private companies. The PRA found its requests for equipment far down on the national priority list. Fortunately, the agency had dozens of warehouses full of supplies left over from a series of depression-era work projects. Mountains of equipment were shipped north, although much of it was not needed or was beyond repair. Finding suitable contractors also proved difficult, although a generous "cost-plus" arrangement attracted suitable interest. Five firms, including one Canadian company, received the major reconstruction contracts. The agencies and companies together supervised the work of 7,500 men in 1942 and over 14,000 in the second year.

The logistical machinery soon broke down. On paper, the Public Roads Administration and U.S. Army Corps of Engineers were to co-operate in construction and planning, with the military retaining supervisory responsibility. In bringing the army's road up to standard, however, the civilian engineers discovered that the route selected for ease of construction was not always suitable for improvement. Although the completed highway was to follow the army's route, the PRA's contractors soon worked along a different, (if parallel) path. While technical advisors argued that such diversions were necessary due to the poor siting of the first road, the failure to co-ordinate construction undermined the efficiency of the two-road plan. Co-operation broke down and acrimonious disputes erupted between the two agencies. The problems were eventually resolved, chiefly by a unilateral American decision to revise the standards for the completed highway downward.

By 1943, much remained to be done. The Alaska Highway was barely a serviceable supply route, let alone a surfaced road. Contractors continued their work of upgrading the pioneer road, relocating sections which could not be maintained, building permanent buildings over major rivers, and struggling with the perpetual problems of permafrost and muskeg. Anxious to open the road to supply convoys, the Army pressured PRA contractors to speed up their work, and allowed even further alterations to the original design. By November 1943, one year after the completion of the pioneer road, the Army declared reconstruction complete. Contractors were released and thousands of imported workers left the area. Most PRA officials also left; a few key members remained behind to assist with highway maintenance.

Considering the problems, the whole episode was an engineering marvel. Over 1,400 miles of highway linking Dawson Creek and Big Delta, Alaska had been completed from survey to reconstruction in less than two years. Yet American officials soon discovered that the work was largely unnecessary, since the anticipated Japanese threat never materialized. Even worse, the navy continued to ship most supplies to Alaska, where many of the settlements could not be reached from the highway. The road did provide a useful, if expensive, link to the airfields of Northwest Staging Route.

The end of construction unleashed an orgy of government waste. It cost too much to ship all the equipment back south and the government was discouraged from selling the materials locally for fear of glutting the local market. Local residents still recall with awe — and anger — the mountains of used materials junked by the Americans. The road itself was an even more lasting legacy of the United States' work. The Canadian government had been promised a properly located, resurfaced road. Although the road was suitable for wartime use, it certainly did not meet civilian standards in many sections.

The CANOL Pipeline Project

Even if the Alaska Highway was not actually required for defence, and proved, from the outset, to be far less than Canadians expected, it at least made for a grand show. The same cannot be said for its companion project, the Canadian Oil (Canol) Pipeline. With the same haste and lack of foresight which had plagued the highway project, the U.S. Army agreed to finance the construction of an oil pipeline between Norman Wells and a refinery to be built in Whitehorse. The plan seemed logical. The supply convoys and airplanes crucial to the defence of the northwest required a secure supply of oil products, and development of refining capacity in the region would reduce dependence on imported oil.

Oil companies and military planners had long known of the Norman Wells reserves. The owner, Imperial Oil, could not justify large-scale commercial production, although a small refinery had been built in the 1930s to supply the Mackenzie River valley market. Hastily organized conferences, involving "experts" who knew little of the special problems of pipeline construction in the middle north, led to an ill-informed decision to proceed. On 30 April 1942, directives were issued for the construction of a 4-inch pipeline and a refinery at Whitehorse. With blinders firmly in place, the Army contracted with several companies, notably field owners Imperial Oil and Standard Oil of California, to start work. Canadian officials saw little logic in the Canol plan, and although a few wondered why Canada simply acquiesced in this American assumption of control over northern resources, the federal government refused to erect any road blocks.

The Americans proceeded with characteristic resolve and a now familiar disregard for cost or efficiency. When drilling near Norman Wells failed to turn up additional oil supplies, the Americans simply requested expanded drilling privileges. (Only when such requests for access to new territories became outrageous did the Canadian government place restrictions on further exploration). Work on the pipeline project began in the spring of 1942 and was completed in 1944. The task was complicated by the difficult terrain and unanticipated problems with pumping the Norman Wells oil.

The project was a fiasco from the outset. Original projections called for a $24 million pipeline and refinery: the actual cost likely exceeded the $134 million in the final U.S. government estimate. Critics in the U.S. did not let this monument to government inefficiency pass unnoticed. A member of the congressional committee investigating the National Defense Program lamented:

> Why didn't we have some good horse trader handling this contract for us [who] would try to make a deal that would be beneficial to our own people who have to foot the bill? I feel we are fighting the war together, and I am of the opinion that we all ought to assume our proportionate share, particularly as this is a Canadian oil development and at the termination of the war Canada will take over, and we have just carried on a gigantic WPA [Works Progress Administration] project for the benefit of the Canadian people, opening up the Canadian wilderness, and Uncle Sam isn't getting anything out of it.

A litany of miscalculations and administrative inefficiencies cast a pall over pipeline construction. In their haste, planners had not consulted reliable authorities on northern conditions. They failed, for example, to note that Norman Wells oil contained high paraffin concentrations which tended to clog the pipelines. Also, a realistic price estimate and a comparison with the costs of alternative supplies would have readily demonstrated the project's financial futility. Even following completion the project proved an embarrassment. Shoddy workmanship and even worker sabotage marred the construction and undermined the efficiency of the pipeline.

Such difficulties and waste could have been brushed aside had the oil proved vital to the war effort. The astonishing cost overruns meant that Norman Wells oil cost over $100 per barrel; comparable products brought by tanker to Skagway and shipped to White-horse via the coastal pipeline cost less than $4 per barrel. The American military's reputation was justi-fiably sullied by the startling revelations of the Congressional Committee. Canol had to go, and in March 1945, only thirteen months after it opened, the system was shut down. The only winners appeared to be Imperial Oil (the major beneficiary of the govern-ment-financed exploration and development programme) and the Canadian government, which wisely refused its option to purchase the pipeline and refinery. At war's end, the Whitehorse refinery was dismantled by Imperial Oil and shipped to the newly opened Leduc field near Edmonton. Two American companies purchased the pipeline itself, which was dismantled and shipped south.

There were more losers. The project left a visible and festering scar across the Canadian northwest. Contractors had displayed little concern for the envi-ronment in their race across the north. After construc-tion, much of the equipment was simply abandoned. Buildings were left to rot, machines, tools, and tele-phone wire to rust away. The right of way itself left a particularly graphic scar. The area would recover slowly from this systematic despoliation. The army's tattered reputation was repaired more easily, for the embarrassment of Canol was erased by the positive reports from the battlefields of World War II. The biggest losers, in financial terms, were the American taxpayers. A small group of over-zealous military planners had committed their country to a project with massive costs, no economic viability, and little military utility.

Northwest Defence and Canadian Sovereignty

By 1944, the three military projects — the staging route, highway, and pipeline — were operational. Only a few minor projects, including a trunk road from the Alaska Highway to Haines, Alaska remained to be completed. While some problems would remain (to be dealt with after the war), the more immediate threat posed by this American-financed-and-supervised construction boom was to Canadian sovereignty. The Canadian government had long neglected its north. Now, in the midst of war, there were numerous signs that the United States had designs on the resources of the northwest. The federal government awakened exceptionally slowly to the threat.

According to local (perhaps apocryphal) legend, receptionists at the U.S. Army's Northwest Command Headquarters answered their phones with "Army of Occupation." Although this threat seems absurd now, in the midst of war it appeared the Americans were preparing for a lengthy stay. The entire northwestern region buzzed with American activity. The sheer numbers of United States personnel, beside which the meagre official Canadian presence paled to insignificance, looked ominous. This, combined with the "Yankees'" chauvinism and unseemly interest in northern resources, set off danger signals. A small number of Canadians, including many in the north and a tiny band of "Northern Nationalists" in Ottawa, tried to alert an uninterested Canadian government to the apparent threat. The Northern Nationalists, many of them senior civil servants, believed that Canada's future lay in the northern latitudes; the Stars and Stripes now visible and proudly flown around the north called those future prospects into question. Most of the fears arose through misunderstanding. Because the Americans planned independently, often informing the Canadian government only after final decisions had been taken, it is easy to see how Canadian civil servants and bureaucrats came to question their neighbour's motives.

The government of William Lyon Mackenzie King was not listening. It was preoccupied with the broader war effort and unwilling to question American intentions. Oddly (and sadly), it was a British diplomat who awakened Canadians' interest and convinced the government to take decisive measures. Malcolm Macdonald, British High Commissioner to Canada and a friend of Prime Minister King, travelled to the north for the first time in 1942. Though his journey was more that of a tourist than a government inspector, it generated in Macdonald a special enthusiasm for Canada's north.

After Macdonald's quick trip, the American presence expanded and the Northern Nationalists clamoured for attention to the neglected region. Perhaps pressured by this interest group, Macdonald returned to the northwest in March 1943. He came back to Ottawa gravely concerned about the massive American presence and the seeming disregard for Canadian sovereignty. Neglecting the strict formalities of his office, Macdonald took his concerns directly to the prime minister. The situation, he alleged, was critical:

[I]t is surely unfortunate that the Canadian authorities have little real say as to, for example, the exact placing of these airfields and the exact route of these roads on Canadian soil. The Americans decide these things according to what they consider American interests. They pay no particular heed to this or that Canadian national or local interest. This aspect of the matter assumes even greater importance when one realises fully the considerations which the American Army, and the other American interests working with them, have in mind in all their efforts in the North-West. Responsible American officers will tell you frankly in confidence that in addition to building works to be of value in this war, they are designing those works also to be of particular value for (a) commercial aviation and transport after the war and (b) waging war against the Russians in the next world crisis.

He warned that unless immediate action was taken, Canada stood to forfeit control of its northland. After long ignoring similar warnings from Canadians, the federal government took Macdonald seriously.

Yet the Canadian response was minimal and bureaucratic. Although conditions obviously called for an assertion of Canadian sovereignty, the politicians and many civil servants still placed the matter fairly low on a long national priority list. The broader vision — that the north held the key to Canada's future — had yet to be accepted.

The response came in two forms: increased supervision of Canadian interests in the north, and plans to take over the defence projects after the war. There had been Canadian liaison officers in the northwest from the beginning of construction, but these junior officers had few powers. The appointment of Brigadier W.W. Foster as Special Commissioner for Defence Projects in the Northwest upgraded significantly the stature of the official federal presence. Armed with fairly sweeping discretionary powers, Foster centralized Canadian decision-making in his Edmonton headquarters and provided for more regular consultation with American project managers. Old patterns proved hard to break, however, and reports of unauthorized American activities surfaced repeatedly. Still, Foster's appointment signalled to the United States and to Canadians that the federal government of Canada finally accepted some of its responsibility in the north.

This public declaration of Canadian interest was matched by behind-the-scenes negotiations with the U.S. government. The original agreement called on the Americans to maintain the Alaska Highway until six months after the war. When the U.S. attempted to reopen negotiations, wanting a guarantee of post-war military access to the highway, Canadian officials wisely rejected the suggestion.

Negotiations on the highway's future continued to run into complications. An American plan to close the Haines Cut-off, contrary to the original agreement (the Canadians claimed), heightened concerns about the United States' commitment to the project. (The federal government also rejected an American request that Canada take over the road before the agreed date, largely because of the unwelcome burden of maintenance costs). Although there was no haste to assume actual responsibility, the federal commitment to the north now had to be maintained, if only for political reasons. An American offer to sell the Canol pipeline was refused, but the Canadian government found money to pay for the Alaska Highway and associated airfields. These cost the government $88.8 million, the bulk of a $123.5 million payment for American improvements and supplies associated with northern defence projects.

The Regional Impact of Military Construction

The entire wartime construction phase had been

conceived, organized, and implemented with little reference to northern Canadians. Although they had little say in the planning, they felt the brunt of the massive "invasion." Special arrangements allowed American military court decisions to take precedence over those of Canadian institutions in cases involving American soldiers. The Canadian government issued hunting licences to U.S. servicemen on duty in the Yukon. This seemingly harmless gesture led to dozens of reports by local residents that the American hunters slaughtered wild game and abandoned the carcasses. The stories grew out of all proportion, culminating in allegations that fighter planes strafed big game animals. Less dramatic, but more controversial, were reports of abandoned women.

Overriding these concerns was the constant tension between regional and military needs. The American Army took over the White Pass and Yukon Route and gave its own supplies top priority. Similarly, organizers diverted most of the sternwheelers on the Yukon River for military use. Civilian needs received remarkably short shrift. Construction materials took precedence over mining supplies and even food. The Canadian government tried to appease local residents by giving Territorial Comptroller George Jeckell authority to negotiate on such matters with the Americans.

Prosperity, combined with a willingess to sacrifice in the interests of the war effort, could overcome such "modest" antagonisms. The military spending promised enough for all. Unfortunately for northern residents, the prosperity was not evenly distributed. Even local bars, the first to profit from the influx of soldiers and labourers, had to contend with strict wartime rationing. Although thousands of men were needed on the highway, most private contractors brought labourers and equipment operators from the south. Local labour representatives complained that the American companies actively discriminated against local workmen. There were jobs in and around the construction sites, and with the businesses which sprung up to serve the workers. Many local companies, particularly in Dawson and Mayo, lost labourers who headed off in search of highway and pipeline work. Yukon Consolidated Gold Corporation, the principal gold mining company, even took the unprecedented step of hiring Indians to work the dredges.

These unusual conditions recast the character of the Yukon. Several Dawson businesses closed down and joined the exodus south to Whitehorse. Whitehorse struggled with the boom, as its limited services were stretched beyond capacity in an attempt to accommodate the thousands of army personnel and labourers. Dawson City remained the nominal capital, but its former dominance now faced a major challenge. The money, population, power, and prestige of highway construction all passed to the southern town, suggesting a major realignment of political and administrative systems. The final changes came after the war, but the accelerated decay of Dawson City and the emergence of Whitehorse were closely tied to wartime activities.

Native people, particularly in the southern Yukon, similarly felt the multi-faceted impact of military construction. Environmental disruptions in the southern Yukon and the unexpected swiftness of construction through previously unopened lands obviously threatened harvesting pursuits. The Indians responded much as they had to earlier flurries of development. A few found short-term positions in the construction camps, typically as guides or labourers. Others (including women), cooked, did laundry, or sold wild meat. The Department of Indian Affairs Agent in the territory tried to take advantage of the new market by encouraging native women to make and sell handicrafts. Those who did found handsome financial rewards, but few took it up on a regular basis.

Most Indians continued to fish, hunt and trap. As several government officials noted, high prices and a consistent demand for furs and meat provided most natives with a decent income, easily equal to wages available in seasonal construction work. Some natives combined the two options. The construction had, on a strictly economic basis, proved of modest importance, with the disruption of game hunting in certain areas offset by the limited opportunities provided with the work crews.

Natives in the southwest corner of the Yukon Territory suffered more directly from highway-related activities. The abundant game in the Kluane Lake region proved particularly enticing to American and Canadian hunters. Concern over permanent damage to game provoked a response from the federal government, which in 1942 closed off to further development a major block of land covering the area between the recently built highway and the Canada-United States border. The Yukon government declared the area a game sanctuary shortly thereafter and suspended even Indian hunting privileges. (The preserve later became Kluane National Park.)

Disease and alcohol had even more obvious impacts than did disruptions of hunting and trapping. C.K. Le Capelain, Canadian liaison officer, reported in 1943:

> The Indians of the Teslin and Lower Post bands until the advent of this new era, have been almost completely

isolated from contacts with white people and, have had the least opportunity of creating an immunity to White peoples' diseases. Consequently they have been distressingly affected by the new contacts....There is no doubt in my mind that if events are allowed to drift along at will, but what the Indian bands at Teslin and Lower Post will become completely decimated within the next few years.

Much like the fur trade routes of the nineteenth century, the Alaska Highway and pipeline access routes served as conduits for imported illnesses. Successive epidemics swept through the Indian camps, striking infants with particular severity. Dozens died, although both Canadian and American medical teams offered aid when possible. The influx of single young men also ensured that natives had greater access to alcohol, often consumed at interracial parties. The high incidence of disease and reports of numerous native arrests for drunkenness (due primarily to more strict enforcement of liquor regulations) encouraged whites to strengthen already existing barriers between natives and the rest of the northern community.

There were other signs, unrelated to wartime construction, that the future held even greater changes. The distress of the 1930s had left its mark and, although as cautious as ever, federal politicians and civil servants sought the means to prevent a post-war return to economic despair. The ''pump-priming'' ideas of John Maynard Keynes caught the attention of policymakers. Selective federal involvement in the economy, many believed, could smooth the wild fluctuations in the private business cycle while leaving the basic capitalist system intact. The war provided an excellent cover for increased federal spending on the kinds of social programmes the reformers advocated.

The passage of the Family Allowance Act in 1944 was the first major sign of this new form of government intervention. The legislation provided all mothers with a monthly subsidy for each child. Even the scattered native population of the Canadian North came under the umbrella of Canada's first universal social aid programme. Even in this new age of apparent enlightenment, vestiges of federal paternalism towards the natives remained. Most Canadians, including natives in the south, received a monthly cheque. Not so for Indians in the north, who received payment in kind. The government did not trust them to spend the money wisely, or on the children.

To ensure the "appropriate" use of the grant, the government authorized traders and Indian Agents to issue the subsidy in practical goods, like canned foods and rubber boots. Also, the allowance was issued only to parents who enrolled their children in school. Although this provision was applied gradually in the north, largely because of the inadequacy of the school system, its later enforcement would have dramatic effects on the natives' nomadic lifestyle.

The challenges emerging during World War II to the natives' way of life remained fairly limited. Indians in the Yukon and southern Mackenzie River regions reacted to the new developments much as they had to earlier booms; new opportunities were integrated as much as possible into hunting and trapping patterns. Events such as the establishment of the Kluane preserve and the introduction of a family allowance pointed to a very different future. If and when the federal government overcame its neglect of the north, it was obvious that the imperatives of southern Canadian society would win out over the lifestyle of the northern harvester.

The rest of the north — beyond the southern Yukon and the upper Mackenzie River valley — was not affected as extensively by the war. Oil drilling expanded beyond the Norman Wells fields, although with few positive results. A series of airstrips was carved out of the forest to expedite the shipment of supplies to exploration and construction projects associated with Canol. Mining activity in the Northwest Territories increased during the war, particularly in the Yellowknife goldfield, although the mines had to compete with military projects for manpower, transportation and supplies.

More modest military developments occurred in the eastern Arctic. In July 1940, the British government had established the North Atlantic Air Ferry route to bring airplanes from manufacturing plants in California to the United Kingdom. Since combat planes and bombers did not yet have the range to fly directly across the Atlantic, a series of airfields connecting the U.S., Canada, Greenland, Iceland, and the British Isles were required. In addition, weather stations were required to provide more accurate forecasts for navigators. The Canadian government again left the task largely to the Americans. Permission was given in 1941 for the United States to develop weather stations at Fort Chimo (in northern Quebec), Frobisher Bay, Baffin Island, and Padloping Island.

As the need for military aircraft in the European theatre of war increased, pressure on the system increased. A new project, code-named "Crimson," was undertaken to build a series of new airfields, divided into an Eastern Section centred on Goose Bay, Newfoundland and a Western Section based in Churchill, Manitoba. The Canadian government authorized construction then stood back while the Americans proceeded with the development of airfields at The Pas, Churchill, Fort Chimo, Coral Harbour on Southampton Island, and Frobisher Bay. As with the Alaska Highway, the enthusiastic American military planners had over-built. As early as 1943 plans were underway to modify and reduce the new system. Reacting to general pressure to reassert its sovereignty, the Canadian government agreed to reimburse the United States for the costs of construction. The stations at The Pas, Churchill and Southampton Island were returned to Canada in April 1945, but the Americans retained control of the more strategically important bases at Fort Chimo and Frobisher Bay until 1949-1950.

Although the projects in the eastern Arctic were on a much smaller scale than the military undertakings in the northwest, the scenario of American initiative and Canadian acquiesence remained in place. Provided these defensive measures did not cost any Canadian money or involve unnecessary commitments, the federal government saw no difficulty in "loaning" its northland to a friendly power.

By assuming control of the highway, guaranteeing its post-war maintenance, and by purchasing the United States' investments in the north, however, the federal government had made an uncharacteristic commitment to the region. Coupled with the emergence of the Canadian welfare state, this pushed and pulled the federal government into an increasingly interventionist role in the Yukon and Northwest Territories. The post-war north would indeed be different.

7
The Bureaucrats' North

The American "invasion" of the Yukon and Northwest Territories during World War II awakened the federal government to its northern responsibilities. Officials in Ottawa had long orchestrated the modest national initiatives for the territories, and the established political systems ensured that civil servants would manage the long-delayed assertion of federal control. The bureaucrats now moved north, although they still adhered to the dictates emanating from the nation's capital. A new north, dominated by new issues but following the familiar colonial path, slowly emerged from the waste and chaos of the wartime construction projects.

The federal government was not alone in finally recognizing the potential of its northern territories. The north was simultaneously popularized by successful authors and promoters. Vilhjalmur Stefannson continued to push his special vision of the Arctic. In a similar vein, author Richard Rohmer's (1960s) concept of the "Mid-Canada Belt" argued that the country's future lay in the often-ignored lands immediately north of the agricultural districts. Even more important in adding flesh to the skeletal images of the northland held by most Canadians were the writings of Pierre Berton and Farley Mowat. Berton's finely-crafted tales of the Klondike revived fading notions of the last great gold rush and, by implication, the north as a land of opportunity. Mowat's various books, including his impassioned (if not always convincing) *Canada's North Now*, emphasized the environmental heritage of the northern territories. His stories stressed man-animal relationships, vividly portraying the minuteness of the human intrusion into the northern landscape.

These writings and others seemed to touch a sensitive nerve, for an expanded market developed for northern literature and commentary. Many of the images remained familiar: the tenuous human hold on the environment, the special Indian and Inuit adaptation, the potential for untold resource riches, and the transient nature of Euro-Canadian settlement. The proliferation of novels, histories and photo-essays revealed a fascination with northern themes not seen since the Klondike gold rush.

The Federal Government and Northern Natives

It was within this context of growing interest in things northern that the federal government increased its involvement in the territories. The heightened activity stemmed, in large part, from a general expansion of government intervention in the economy and society, as the federal government slowly expanded the welfare state initiatives begun during World War II. When the federal government finally looked north after 1945, therefore, they did so from a new perspective. The politicians were prepared to spend money, lead economic development if necessary, and extend services to those most in need.

While the welfare state expanded slowly for most Canadians, assistance for native people was more forthcoming. By the mid-1950s, the federal government began to enforce more strictly the provisions of the Mother's Allowance. The native day school programme was expanded and efforts were made in larger communities to integrate Indian students into territorial schools. Parents now had to choose: to stay in the settlement during the school year and receive the monthly payments, or continue nomadic patterns and forfeit the subsidy. With returns from the fur trade dropping rapidly, many families felt they had little choice.

Other programmes were more deliberately interventionist. The poor health of northern natives was a matter of particular concern. Beginning in 1947, federal medical officers conducted extensive tuberculosis testing among both native and white residents. The tests confirmed the government's worst fears — dozens of natives had advanced tuberculosis, requiring immediate hospitalization.

Although medically and legally sound (the latter because the government granted itself special powers), the insistence that people be sent ''outside'' had traumatic social implications. The new tuberculosis wing at the Whitehorse General Hospital could not handle the influx of patients, so most Yukon clients were sent to Edmonton. Natives elsewhere in the north were similarly sent to other southern centres; the health care was unquestionably better than that available in the north, but the patients were a long way from home. Many never returned.

The commitment to native health went beyond this survey and hospitalization programme. The Department of Indian Affairs and the newly created Department of National Health and Welfare hired nurses, doctors, and dentists to visit settlements and provide emergency and preventive care. Distance precluded many natives from having access to these services, but as the Indians and Inuit moved into the larger settlements for schooling or work, more came under the government's net.

Native education similarly underwent major changes in the 1950s and 1960s. The government finally decided in the 1950s to apply, in the north, the assimilationist values that formed the philisophical foundation of national Indian policy. Where possible (particularly in the Yukon), native children were enrolled in existing white schools. By offering native children the standard Canadian curriculum, the government hoped to speed their assimilation into the broader Canadian society.

Most natives remained beyond the reach of the modest territorial school systems, which operated only in the major towns and mining camps. Therefore, students from the outlying districts were placed in residential schools. Modern buildings replaced the old quarters, and missionaries gradually lost control of the programme although they continued to participate in administration and teaching. The revitalized residential schools proved even more disruptive than their forerunners, thanks to a strict assimilationist programme. The children, taken from family and community at a young age, suffered considerable cultural alienation. Then, at the time of graduation, they were expected to return to their communities and fit back into a way of life they had learned to disdain. Largely in response to native protests, the residential programmes had fallen from favour by the late 1950s. Such schools remain in several centres, such as Inuvik, where children from isolated communities are educated (usually in advanced grades).

The new wave of federal intervention extended beyond an expansion of existing initiatives. Shortly after the war, the government started a modest subsidy programme for native-owned businesses. As R.J. Meek, Indian Agent for the Yukon, reported in 1949, "Whenever possible, financial aid is given to Indians to assist them in possible worthwhile fields of endeavour, in preference to direct relief." Most subsidies involved loans to buy trucks or heavy equipment or to start a small service business. This programme and others like it attempted to train natives to adapt to the industrial system. Given the limited job prospects and continuing job discrimination against native workers, such measures offered only short-term support.

More imaginative regional approaches enjoyed greater success. In recognition of the limited economic opportunities available to Arctic residents, the federal government encouraged the development of Inuit co-operatives. Several such ventures opened in the late 1950s, sustained initially by federal grants. The co-operatives drew on the communal orientation of much Inuit work and also provided an opportunity for economic self-sufficiency within the capitalist market. The government assisted the process in several ways — for instance, by closing federally-run stores in such places as Resolute Bay and Grise Fiord to make way for the co-operatives. The new stores proved particularly responsive to local needs, soon emerging as important competitors to the HBC in the fur trade. Twelve co-operative stores operated in the Arctic in 1968, mostly in the eastern Arctic islands and Keewatin. Several of the co-operatives, prodded by government officials, began marketing Inuit artifacts. The distinctive Inuit carvings and prints, which sit well on the coffee table next to Berton's or Mowat's books, found a ready market. By the 1970s, the sale of artwork had become a major component of the Inuit economy. Many of the co-operatives, active in fur trading and the sale of art, became self-supporting. The experience in local control, management, and Inuit assertiveness proved an important training ground for Inuit politicians as well.

The changes in federal programming for natives — more money, more civil servants, and many new programmes — all reflected national priorities rather than a specific response to northern problems. In a sense, the missionary zeal of earlier decades had been bureaucratized and transferred to the Department of Indian Affairs.

The Federal Government and the Northern Economy

In other areas, particularly economic development, the government did come up with new northern policies. The plans emerged slowly, partially because of more pressing southern concerns, but more because few policy makers yet had a clear notion of the north's future role. Canada had, after all, been rudely awakened to its northern responsibilities during the war. The country had decided to assert its sovereignty; it had not yet decided what to do with the land.

The administration of the Alaska Highway illustrates most graphically the evolving federal attitude to the north. Many civilians, attracted by the stories of war-time propagandists, eagerly awaited the post-war opening of the highway. The government procrastinated, somewhat embarrassed to reveal the poorly-sited, rough road. The road remained closed to civilian traffic after the Canadian Army assumed control of the highway in April 1946. Without adequate equipment or funds, the Army could undertake only patch-work repairs, not the major reconstruction that was required.

The government partially lifted the traffic restrictions in 1948, although they maintained tight regulations to ensure that travellers were adequately prepared for the arduous and costly journey.

Although the inevitable adventure-seekers toured the highway, it could not compete with the White Pass and Yukon Route Railway as a shipping route. The military retained control of the highway, ostensibly for use in a training programme for its engineers. The road was maintained and new camps were built along the highway. But to northern residents it was obvious that with the Army in place, no upgrading would occur.

The regional position received a major boost in 1961, when a report prepared by the Batelle Memorial Institute called for the immediate paving of the highway, which it saw as the cornerstone of economic development in the northwest. Northerners rejoiced when, on 1 April 1964, the federal Department of Public Works assumed control of the highway. But the federal government wished to turn over responsibility for the highway to the appropriate territorial or provincial authority as soon as possible.

Demands for an improved highway mounted during the 1960s. The federal government responded, typically, by commissioning an economic feasability study. The Stanford Research Institute's report was much more restrained than the earlier Batelle study. It called for a modest reconstruction programme aimed, in the long run, at improving the entire route. The report offered a politically palatable solution, for it permitted the government to adopt a formal policy of reconstruction but freed it to proceed on a yearly basis as funds and political will dictated. Thus the Department of Public Works' reconstruction programme, begun in 1968, gave the appearance of great action without formal commitment to large-scale work or an early completion. The resulting patch-work highway, with stretches of unimproved highway broken by reconstructed road of the highest quality, only partially mollified people in the region.

The centralization and upgrading of administrative control over the complex range of northern matters hinted at greater federal interest than did its attitude to the highway. Before the war, sub-departments, like the Mining Lands and Yukon Branch (established in 1906), NWT and Yukon Branch (1922), and Northern Administration Branch (1951) managed the country's northern activities. The new post-war environment inspired the creation of a Department of Northern Affairs and National Resources in 1953. A further rationalization of related government services led to the establishment of the Department of Indian Affairs and Northern Development in 1961. This latter move seemed to put the wolves in with the chickens, in that the department's responsibilities to defend native interests were often directly at odds with the priorities of would-be developers. The bureaucratic shuffling reflected the emerging political importance of northern and native issues and also gave sharper administrative focus to regional planning.

Attention to the north peaked during the Diefenbaker years, 1957-1963. When John Diefenbaker approached the Canadian electorate in 1958 with his ''Vision'' of a new Canada, he opened a new phase in the public consideration of the north. The Conservative leader called on Canadians to cut the umbilical cord which tied them to the United States and to cast their eyes northward. This vast, undeveloped land, he argued, held the key to Canada's future. He spoke eloquently and passionately of the north, much as John A.

Macdonald had described the west in the previous century. Diefenbaker accordingly called his plan for northern development the "New National Policy," harkening back to the nationalistic and expansionist ideas of the Old Chieftain.

Canadians embraced both the man and his vision. Never before had the northern regions occupied such a central place in the country's development plans. It was time for the promoters, who had long begged for government attention to their region, to demonstrate the north's true potential.

While it made for fine rhetoric, Diefenbaker's northern vision proved difficult to translate into official policy. Alvin Hamilton, Minister of Northern Affairs and National Resources, orchestrated the planning for economic revival. In its early conception, the plan included a massive northern road building campaign to provide access to resources, aid for new railways, scientific exploration in the Arctic, and a development scheme for the town of Frobisher Bay on Baffin Island. Hamilton's conception was not unlike that of earlier northern promoters; the north, he said, "represents a new world to conquer - [and] it is much more than that. It is like a great vault, holding in its recesses treasures to maintain and increase the material living standards which our countries take for granted." The old image of the northern treasure trove, to be tapped for southern use, had re-emerged.

Hamilton, one of the more competent members of the Conservative cabinet, soon gave practical expression to his leader's vision. He had his department's budget enlarged, and expanded its role in the identification and development of resources. There was greater assistance for northern residents, particularly natives, but the emphasis remained on exploiting natural resources. The government's financial commitment was evident in its Territorial Roads and "Roads to Resources" programmes, support for scientific investigations, improvements to northern communication, subsidies for a railway to Pine Point on Great Slave Lake, and other efforts to open up the north. Private investors received ample encouragement; new oil and gas regulations, for example, opened millions of acres in the Yukon and Northwest Territories for exploration.

Long-standing northern criticism of federal policies abated in the wave of federally-sponsored activities. If the burst of government involvement under Hamilton from 1958 to 1960 characterized the new southern commitment to the north, the region's future seemed secure.

Turmoil within the Conservative cabinet forced the Prime Minister to shift Hamilton to the Department of Agriculture in 1960, removing the chief architect and promoter of the new north. Diefenbaker tried to rekindle the vision in the election campaign of 1962, but the promises sounded stale, coming as they did on the heels of four years of political chaos. The Conservatives clung to power for a year with a minority government, but in 1963 were defeated by a modestly reinvigorated Liberal Party led by Lester B. Pearson. Interest in northern issues receded over the next decade.

The inability to maintain Hamilton's impressive pace with northern development schemes was not due entirely to Conservative ineptness. The north had, in a sense, failed the politicians. Grandiose descriptions of untapped resources raised unrealistic expectations. Although a few mines opened and other activities increased, particularly in the northern regions of the central and western provinces, the vault of which

Hamilton had spoken was, in fact, rather bare. The resources were there, but they were not as abundant or easy to extract as anticipated. The government and developers were discovering the limits on what the north could produce.

It was only in this post-war period, however, that Canadians at least began to explore the limits of the region's potential. Southern Canadians had long questioned the possibility of diversifying from the narrow fur trade and mining base. A few promoters tried to offset the general pessimism with eloquent testimonials to the north's resources. The reality obviously lay between these extremes.

The expanded economy rested on the established base of fur trading and small-scale mining. Although of continued importance to natives, the fur industry lost much of its vitality when prices collapsed after 1947. Individual returns fell off dramatically in real dollars. As late as 1948, the fur trade accounted for more than 20 per cent of territorial output; by the 1960s, the figure was around 3 per cent.

The government made several changes to protect the natives' position and to conserve a declining resource base. Both the Northwest Territories, in 1949, and the Yukon, in 1950, instituted individual and group trapline registration. Natives and mixed bloods were given first claim to trapping districts. The project had laudable goals, but the execution proved flawed. Northern natives seldom considered traplines to be personal property; they were instead held by a family or community. Although some traplines were registered on a group basis, the majority were allocated to individuals, usually men. This in turn caused problems, for native tradition throughout the north rested on maternal inheritance. In one single bureaucratic sweep, the government cast aside an age-old pattern and injected new tensions into an already threatened native society.

The formation of the Yukon Fish and Game Association in 1945 signalled the arrival of contemporary North American conservation attitudes in the north. The association's advocacy led to the appointment of a director of game and publicity, an unlikely hybrid reflecting the perception that Yukon game could be marketed in the south. The YFGA convinced territorial officials to ban the commercial sale of wild game, a direct attack on an important part of the native economy. Although advocates claimed these and other measures were required to protect endangered species, the regulations reflected southern values more than regional realities.

The fur trade continued, notwithstanding these new, aggressively implemented measures. Many white trappers had been driven out by the poor market conditions of the 1950s. The natives often chafed against the new regulations, protesting such charges as the annual $10 trapline fee imposed in the Yukon in 1950. The town-based government programmes, schools and subsidies drew some natives away from the harvesting economy, but most continued in the trade on at least a part-time basis. The Family Allowances, welfare payments and other federal assistance programmes offset the steadily declining trapline returns. With the natives and mixed bloods maintaining their harvesting practice, the fur trade was assured a continued, if diminished, importance in the northern economy.

On the territorial balance sheet, a surge in mining activity compensated for the decline in the fur trade. Pre-war production (excluding the gold rush) peaked at nearly $6.3 million in 1942. Rising mineral prices and the development of new properties pushed the value of territorial mineral production over $32 million by 1954. The marked increase only hinted at what lay ahead, for over the next two decades the industry diversified beyond its base in the Dawson, Keno, and Yellowknife areas. Awakened to the north's potential — enhanced by increased federal assistance for frontier development — Canadian and foreign companies poured millions of dollars into the formerly neglected region.

The Yukon mining industry rebounded slowly from the disappointments of the war years. With labour once again available, Yukon Consolidated Gold Corporation resurrected its Klondike dredging operations. But falling gold prices threatened the viability of this and other gold properties, forcing the federal government to rescue the industry with the 1947 Emergency Gold Mining Assistance Act. YCGC finally stopped production in 1966, leaving the goldfields to the tourists. Only an unprecedented surge in gold prices in the late 1970s could bring a number of small-scale miners back to the diggings.

The Mayo-Keno mines underwent similar changes. Treadwell Yukon Company had closed its operations in 1943. Then high post-war prices renewed interest in the ore-body and the Keno Hill Mining Company bought the Treadwell holdings. Reorganized as United Keno Hill in 1947, the company reopened the old mine, modernized operations, and improved transportation to the isolated site. Government price subsidies, as well as assistance with hydro development and highway construction, helped make the firm viable. This pattern of entrepreneurial initiative bolstered by government aid soon became a familiar one.

Several new mines also came on stream, signalling what seemed a new era of diversified production and renewed prosperity. The discovery of an asbestos property near Dawson led to the creation of the town of Clinton Creek near the new mine. A large lead/silver/zinc deposit on the Anvil-Dynasty property (later Cypress Anvil) in the central Yukon was developed, as was the nearby townsite of Faro. Copper properties near Whitehorse and a tungsten deposit in the Mackenzie Mountains northwest of Watson Lake were also turned into operating mines.

The mining boom sent expectations sky-rocketting. Mineral production rose and spin-off benefits led to a major business expansion in Whitehorse to service the mines. Prospects looked bright throughout the 1960s as periodic announcements of further discoveries and the start-up of small-scale mines reinforced the image of a prosperous and diversified regional mining economy. Although the industry remained structurally unstable due to its dependence on world market conditions, the mines appeared to offer the territory economic security and a bright future.

Conditions in the Northwest Territories were even more positive, particularly compared to the small-scale pre-war operations. As in the Yukon, gold production suffered during the war; the Yellowknife mines had all but closed down by 1944. The field expanded rapidly after the war. Several of the properties, including Con, Ryan, Grant, Negus and the rich Discovery, became producing mines. Gone too were the impermanent mining camps. Each of the major properties employed several hundred men, and with their wives and children they formed the basis of a more stable community.

While the Yellowknife properties dominated territorial production, interest in northern mining extended beyond the goldfields. The Canadian government expropriated the Port Radium pitchblende mines in 1944, primarily in an attempt to ensure that the Canadian government gained control over supplies of the uranium ore required for military research and development. The Port Radium mines were operated as a Crown corporation, Eldorado Nuclear, until their closure in 1960.

The Pine Point development on the southern shore of Great Slave Lake was far more impressive. The existence of a large, low-grade lead/zinc ore-body had been known for many years, but high production costs scared off would-be promoters. After World War II, the property's owners, Consolidated Mining and Smelting Corporation, began more detailed work on the reserve. Drilling tests revealed considerable high-grade ore, but the company balked at the high transportation costs. Federal authorities, (after delays for suitable studies by a government commission), announced in 1961 that an $86 million subsidy, supplemented by $12.5 million from the mine developers, had been authorized for the construction of the Great Slave railway. Work started the next year on both the rail-line and the mine property.

A few other properties, including a nickel/copper mine near Rankin Inlet and another Cominco mine at Nanisivik on Baffin Island were developed. A unique ocean-borne concentrating plant was barged to the mine site, built in such a fashion that it could be towed away when the ore-body is worked out. Inuit workers who were recruited from throughout the Keewatin to work at the short-lived Rankin Inlet mine, faced severe hardship when the mine closed, being far away from their former homes, and without work in their new community. Although the new mines added to regional production and led an economic expansion outside the Mackenzie River basin, the projects were too small in scale to match post-war expectations for the far north.

Many hoped that oil resources in the middle north and Arctic would bring the long-touted prosperity. Wartime interest in northern petroleum, although tainted by the Canol debacle, convinced a number of companies to step up exploration. The government encouraged this revived interest, easing regulations and issuing drilling leases covering over 25 million acres by the mid-1950s. Initial work concentrated in the Mackenzie River valley, but exploration soon expanded into the northern Yukon. Disappointing early results tempered the enthusiasm, but a push to the Arctic coast and islands in the early 1960s kept interest alive. A few minor discoveries hinted at the region's oil potential, but a major strike remained elusive.

Events outside the region sparked renewed interest in northern petroleum in the 1970s. Increasing demand, higher prices, and irregularity of world supply forced the oil companies to look to the Canadian North. What had before been marginal properties of little value suddenly were inviting. The Canadian government created Panarctic Oils Ltd. in 1967 to lead exploration in the Arctic islands, but the first major northern strike lay elsewhere. The discovery of huge oil reserves at Prudhoe Bay in northern Alaska in 1968 convinced exploration companies to shift their emphasis to the Mackenzie Delta and Beaufort Sea while work continued in the islands. When Imperial Oil discovered oil near Tuktoyaktuk in 1970, northern production seemed a very real prospect, and drilling activity increased accordingly.

The oil was in the ground; fields at Prudhoe Bay, Tuktoyaktuk and Norman Wells demonstrated that.

The problem was getting it to market. After the voyages of the American tanker *Manhattan* in 1969-1970 (another affront to Canadian sovereignty that the country did not respond to effectively) demonstrated that west-east Arctic Ocean shipping was not feasible, attention turned to a series of competing pipeline proposals. Canadian politicians, believing the optimistic forecasts of northern oil promoters, advocated connecting the Prudhoe Bay field with known and potential territorial wells. Plans foundered in 1972 when the Americans selected a trans-Alaskan route. With the OPEC oil crisis the following year, northern Canadian reserves were suddenly of prime importance, and talk of multi-billion-dollar pipelines dominated plans for the expansion of the northern economy.

The Canadian government encouraged the frontier development with an attractive package of subsidies and tax incentives. The logic behind these multi-billion-dollar concessions to the oil companies was that northern oil discoveries would stimulate both the northern and national economies and also satisfy the Liberal government's determination to make Canada self-sufficient in petroleum. To spearhead this drive toward Canadian self-sufficiency, and as a standard-bearer for the Liberals' newly-discovered Canadianization policy, PetroCanada was created in 1975. This new arm of government was given preferential drilling rights in the north to ensure an active federal presence in the northern oil patch.

The creation of PetroCanada was the first hint of the new direction in energy policy. Anxious to grab the lion's share of royalties and profits from the as yet undiscovered northern fields, the Liberal government announced a National Energy Programme in October 1980, promising self-sufficiency in a decade and greater

Canadian control of the oil industry. The Canadian Oil and Gas Act guaranteed the federal government a "back-in" provision, allowing Ottawa to claim 25 per cent ownership of any producing well discovered on leased land. The act also provided hefty incentives for any companies with more than 50 per cent Canadian ownership. Dome Petroleum was the prime beneficiary of this new federal initiative, as it both met the federal guidelines and was a major player in Arctic exploration.

The plan was a disaster from the beginning, in part because of unfortunate timing: the legislation coincided with a sharp downturn in oil prices. But the principal fault was the government's heavy-handed treatment of the oil industry. Companies cancelled or postponed development plans, and anger mounted over Ottawa's allegedly confiscatory measures. By the early 1980s, conditions had turned sour. Dome Petroleum, the darling of the Liberal party's Canadianization scheme, continued to issue optimistic press releases, but they could not prevent the company's imminent financial collapse. Dome Petroleum almost went under, and would have probably taken several of Canada's largest financial institutions with it, had not the Liberal government stepped in to bail the company out.

The flurry of oil-related activity reflected all too well the drawbacks of the standard pattern of frontier development. After decades of neglect, the south had "discovered" northern oil and rushed — with ample government encouragement — to develop the resource. Again, there was little concern for regional interests. The territorial governments were among the strongest opponents of the new federal oil legislation because no additional revenues flowed directly to the north. Indeed, it was only in the colonies, where the government retained unchallenged constitutional supremacy, that such interventionist measures could even be contemplated. As the initial glow wore off, and business and government took a more rational look at the costs and problems associated with northern oil development, the boom rapidly turned to a bust. Pipeline proposals were shelved or modified; plans for large-scale development were reduced or dropped entirely. The north had been told to plan for a boom and had done so. The region was left almost alone to pick up the pieces of another northern vision gone sour.

Frontier oil exploration and post-war mining also typified the new, bureaucratic pattern of northern development. Both relied on extensive government assistance. The development companies had, in effect, helped in the bureaucratization of the north by requesting or even demanding federal aid before starting production. Northern businesses had bitterly claimed that they received little government assistance. In the post-war period, the appeal for federal aid had become an integral part of the development process. The assistance was often forthcoming, in the form of tax incentives, direct subsidies, cost-sharing programmes, favourable legislation, and help with transportation.

The federal hand was particularly evident in the development of rail, road and communication systems. Dawson and Whitehorse were linked by an all-weather road in 1953, undermining the viability of riverboat travel, which ended in 1955. New highways, usually built on a cost-sharing basis, joined the mines at Clinton Creek, Can-Tung, Faro, Pine Point and elsewhere with existing roads. The Development Road programme led to work on the Dempster Highway linking Dawson City and Inuvik, and a road joining Fort Smith to Fort Simpson and Yellowknife. Existing airfields were upgraded and communication networks were developed to provide contact between previously isolated communities.

The Dempster Highway remained a short access road until a major extension was announced in 1965. The project was not completed until 1978. The launching of a special Anik satellite in the early 1970s greatly improved northern telecommunications and brought live television to the region. Northerners occasionally argued about the pace of development or specific federal priorities, but they generally applauded the new commitment to territorial services. These government initiatives unfolded slowly, although the net result of public sector investment in the post-war period was quite impressive.

The North and Continental Defence

The Canadian government was not alone in its new-found interest in the northern territories. In the tense years of the Cold War, the United States rediscovered the Arctic. Post-war fears of the suddenly aggressive Russian ''Bear,'' armed with long-range bombers, raised new questions about continental defence. Canada felt compelled to stand beside the United States in the gathering confrontation and agreed to a series of joint defence projects. Only two years after the war, joint U.S.-Canada weather stations were opened at Resolution, Eureka Sound, Mould Bay, Isachsen, and Alert. Frobisher Bay was developed as a strategic air base, complete with expanded airfields and communications capacities.

The sheer enormity of the Canadian North and the prospect of an unexpected Soviet air attack posed an urgent problem. The Mid-Canada line of radar stations, built roughly along the 55th parallel, addressed the threat partially, but military advisors in the United States said that more was necessary. Some form of early warning system was essential, but northern climatic and magnetic conditions rendered existing radar devices ineffective. When scientific advances improved radar technology, construction began on the $400 million Distant Early Warning (DEW) Line, a network of fifty-eight radar stations stretching from Alaska to Baffin Island. Financed and manned in the main by the U.S., the DEW Line was to provide an impenetrable radar shield.

The system was almost immediately outdated. By the late 1950s, refinements in missile technology allowed the Russians to point long-range inter-continental ballistic missiles at North American targets. The launching of surveillance satellites further negated the value of the Arctic defence network. With warning times now calculated in minutes rather than hours, the expensive DEW Line lost its primary value. Many stations were abandoned, and the region was downgraded from the first line of defence to a training and testing ground. Even the modest Canadian army and airforce establishments remaining in Whitehorse after the war were withdrawn in the late 1960s, although a small northern defence headquarters was opened in Yellowknife in 1970.

The combination of military investment, expanded mineral and oil exploration, the fur trade, and a greatly expanded tourism industry, all increased the scale if not the shape of the northern economy. There were more mines, but territorial subservience to external markets and the financial stability of southern companies remained. The increased federal involvement was welcomed, but the vagaries of national politics ensured that northern affairs were not always a government priority.

Society in the "New" North

The Yukon and Northwest Territories had long been bicultural societies, divided between native districts and small enclaves of predominately white settlement. The white population had typically been highly transient, tied to the sojourner mentality of making money and returning home. In large measure, the post-war communities retained this structure. The government sent large numbers of civil servants north and their arrival recast several northern towns. The population of both territories more than doubled between 1951 and 1976, from 9,000 to almost 22,000 in the Yukon and from 16,000 to more than 42,000 in the Northwest Territories.

Despite the influx of whites to the mines, construction camps and government centres, most of the increase came from the native population. Vastly improved health care and a sharp decrease in infant mortality aided the rise. Over the 1951-1976 period, the native population (status and non-status) increased from 2,200 to 6,000 in the Yukon. In the Northwest Territories, the combined Indian, Metis and Inuit population grew from 13,000 to 24,000.

The changes in the north are symbolized by the tale of two cities: Whitehorse and Yellowknife. At war's end, the two were boom towns, Whitehorse enjoying the last phase of Alaska Highway construction and Yellowknife poised at the centre of a high-grade goldfield. The future held a different course for the two towns.

The war years had created a shift of power from Dawson to Whitehorse, but the old capital tried to compete with the road, river and rail entrepôt. Dawson residents and political representatives fought to preserve the town's position, asking in particular for a highway to join Dawson with a road being built between Mayo and Whitehorse. The battle was lost. A federal government building was erected in Whitehorse in 1952 and the following year the territorial capital was relocated in the southern city.

Whitehorse was now the cornerstone of the Yukon, its prominence resting on its role as a transportation centre. The army built a self-contained ''southern'' suburb on the escarpment overlooking the town centre. Other government departments followed with housing developments for their employees, giving a large part of the town a southern, white collar cast. Whitehorse had long been a company town, first of the White Pass and Yukon Route and later of the United States Army. Now the company was the federal government.

In the years after it became the territorial capital, Whitehorse underwent a remarkable transformation. Paved streets, the new residential suburb, new schools, government office buildings, improved sewage and water systems, a new city hall (built as a centennial project), a medium-security prison, a large library, a modern hospital, and a power dam all changed the World War II boom town into a fragment of southern Canada. Many of the amenities of southern Canadian life — more in fact than most cities of comparable size — were available in town. Business expanded, both to serve the largely middle-class residents and the growing regional economy. Although the northern setting ensured a special community character, one particularly evident during the annual Sourdough Rendezvous, the town's civil service orientation shone clearly through.

Yellowknife similarly passed from a mining centre to a government centre. Following the advice of the Carrothers Commission on the constitutional evolution of the Northwest Territories, the federal government transferred the territories' administrative offices from Ottawa to Yellowknife in 1967. As the new capital, the town quickly assumed the trappings of a government centre, complete with office buildings, new housing developments, an expanded service sector, and, to fill the new regional departments, hundreds of imported civil servants. By the late 1970s, over 3,000 territorial and 1,000 federal bureaucrats worked in the territory, most of them in the capital city.

The bureaucratization extended throughout the north. New schools opened in most communities, local governments were established, and administrative personnel responsible for game management, land regulations, vital statistics, highway maintenance, national parks and tourism appeared in centres throughout the north. Medium-sized regional centres, particularly Dawson City, Inuvik, and Frobisher Bay provide graphic evidence of the impact of government programming on social development. Parks Canada's massive investment in the Dawson Historic Site project revitalized the gold rush town as a tourist attraction. Much of the work and most of the workers remained seasonal, but the programme doubtlessly saved the community from ignominious disintegration.

The south soon had a new northern image to add to its collection: Inuvik was created in the 1950s as an administrative centre for the western Arctic. The town was built above ground, its buildings connected by the distinctive ''utilidors'' which carry water and heating conduits above ground to prevent disruptions due to the permafrost. The government hoped that concentrating a variety of federal and territorial services in a modern community would draw in the Indian and Inuit population, and thus allow government programmes to have full effect. It did not work as planned, since most of the natives stayed away, but the expansion of Arctic oil exploration made the town a business centre. Frobisher Bay had been initially built by the United States Army as a weather station and airfield, and retained its military role into the 1950s. As the Canadian federal presence in the north expanded, the town became the adminstrative centre for the eastern Arctic.

The social impact of this bureaucratization, recent as it is, is difficult to gauge. Although northerners welcomed federal attention to their concerns and applauded in particular the expansion of territorially-run activities, the importation of thousands of white southerners to manage the north occasionally grated. As Louis-Edmond Hamelin noted, the pain was not always in one direction:

> In the majority of the settlements, where the phenomena of isolation, underdevelopment, and an indigenous majority predominate, the administrators, the bulk of whom are White, have been faced with psychological, administrative and cultural problems. Fortunately, until now, the forces of tension have been mainly latent.

Civil servants proved only slightly less transient than other sojourners. They were shifted from job to job by their federal bosses, and themselves often viewed a stint in the north as a stepping-stone to a better career. The creation of government residential enclaves, particularly in Whitehorse and Yellowknife, highlighted the difference between permanent residents and civil servants. Most important, perhaps, the southerners demanded and received the accoutrements of home, ensuring that climate and isolation remained almost the only vestiges of the towns' northern situation. Yet not all the southerners succumbed to the protection of their suburban enclaves; many civil servants became northerners, drawn by the land, people and possibilities of the north.

Other northern company towns resembled scaled-down versions of the capitals and regional centres. The larger mines, such as Pine Point, Clinton Creek, and Faro, differed greatly from earlier operations. Faced with a more assertive trade union movement and the difficulty of attracting skilled tradespeople to isolated northern communities, the companies created comfortable, middle-class towns for their workers. Amenities like curling rinks, schools, hospitals, hotels, bars, and subsidized trips "outside" were tossed in as added enticements. Even so, cheap housing, high wages, and extensive services were not always enough. The mining camps remained extremely transient, with a small core of long-term residents surrounded by dozens of sojourners. The communities remained essentially incomplete, with single men typically far outnumbering single women, and social life characterized by excessive drinking and drug use. Even the towns themselves were not permanent. Shortly after the Clinton Creek mine closed, the houses were sold and trucked away, leaving little trace of the several hundred people who once lived there.

Many of the high-grade gold mines and the Beaufort Sea oil rigs operate now with an even less permanent workforce. Imported crews work on a cycle of six weeks in, six weeks out (or some variation of this). While in the north, the men and women remain on-site, working long hours, then retreat to the cloistered security of the small "bubbles" of southern comfort in their quarters. Their internment is only temporary, though, as they regularly fly south to Edmonton, Calgary, Saskatoon, or Vancouver — back to civilization. Although technically northern workers, such individuals leave no appreciable impression on the society through which they pass.

The native peoples stand at the opposite pole from these transient workers. Post-war society has retained much of its earlier bicultural and segregationist nature. Government programmes, particularly reserve housing projects, compulsory education, and welfare, have brought more natives into the towns. In some areas, like the Arctic and much of the Mackenzie River valley, natives dominated the small settlements — places such as Fort McPherson, Fort Simpson, Fort Good Hope, Frobisher Bay, Baker Inlet, and Spence Bay in the Northwest territories; and Old Crow, Burwash, and Ross River in the Yukon. Here most of the whites are police officers, missionaries, teachers, Indian Agents, and other government officials. The communities retain their essentially native character.

In the larger centres and mining camps, racial distinctions remain very much in evidence. Natives tend to live outside the white residential areas, often in government housing. The integrated education system brought native and white children together in schools, but the imperatives of the white, southern curriculum ensured that attrition filtered out most native students by the senior secondary years. There were few jobs for natives in the towns and mines. Some, barred from employment by discriminatory policies, and no longer able to trap profitably (due to over-hunting and low prices), turned to readily available government subsidies. There were other options. For instance, many communities in the Northwest Territories and, by the 1980s, a few settlements in the Yukon, opened producer and consumer co-operatives.

Although the co-operative movement brought some positive changes, most aspects of the new north held little attraction for the natives. Declining fur prices and the introduction of southern, conservationist values that ended most market hunting cut into their income severely. Extended government intervention, paternalistic and disruptive, forced even further changes in lifestyle and occupation. Capping it all, when the long-awaited development explosion finally arrived, the whites seemed intent on shouldering the natives aside.

Buffeted by economic reorganization, government intervention, and social pressures, Indian and Inuit societies underwent dramatic changes. Federal attempts to establish reserve housing failed miserably in most quarters. The homes were often inappropriate, built to suit southern standards rather than northern conditions. Little attention was given to water services or sanitation, and overcrowding was endemic. The increasing dependence on government hand outs undermined native self-esteem, leading in turn to severe alcohol problems, considerably high rates of native crime, and further tensions between the native and white communities. Native culture appeared under attack from all quarters, as the acculturative demands of the school system also challenged traditional native learning and undermined the position of community elders. The problems were particularly acute in the larger centres, where the squalor of the native people stood in stark contrast to the middle-class comforts enjoyed by most whites. This is not as true in isolated communities, where the continued importance of harvesting has enabled the natives to resist many of the changes. The plan for the "new" north, however, assigned the natives to a peripheral role, rendering them more an impediment than a partner in the economic boom.

The Rise of Northern Native Activism

The rapid pace of development generated a native response in the form of Indian and Inuit activism. In the political maelstrom of the 1960s, minority rights gained national and international prominence. Long-neglected aboriginal rights finally gained a measure of importance for government and politicians.

The Canadian government unwittingly encouraged this development with the introduction in 1969 of a White Paper on Indian Affairs. This ill-conceived document promised natives the opportunity for full participation in Canadian cultural, social, economic, and political life. Specific proposals called for the elimination of the Department of Indian Affairs, the transfer to the provinces of many responsibilities for Indian affairs, the repeal of the Indian Act, and additional funds for economic development. Drafted without consultation with native leaders, the proposals received a rough ride from native organizations. Natives saw shifts in responsibility as ominous so long as land claims and other issues remained unresolved, and regarded the White Paper as an attempt to destroy native society as it currently existed. The furor over the government's proposals touched off a wave of native rights advocacy. Southern activists, like the Company of Young Canadians and representatives of the Anglican Church of Canada, brought the concerns of the national native rights movement to the Canadian north (although this intervention sometimes impeded the emergence of local leaders). By the mid-1970s, however, highly motivated northern native organizations had entered into negotiations with the federal government.

They had a lot to talk about. The Yukon Indians and the Inuit had never been taken into treaty by the federal government, and their outstanding land claims remained to be addressed. The natives of the Mackenzie River valley had accepted a treaty in 1921, and although the settlement was more imposed than negotiated, they had not received the promised reserves.

The Yukon Native Brotherhood started formal discussions in 1973 with the release of *Together Today for Our Children Tomorrow*, a compehensive claim demanding both financial and land compensation. The native organization, renamed the Council for Yukon Indians and broadened to incorporate non-status Indians, reached a tentative settlement in 1976. The proposal, which would have granted Indians between seventy and ninety million dollars and specific land and hunting rights, was repudiated by the council's membership. Negotiators were told to start again, this time with a specific directive to aim for an agreement guaranteeing native peoples an equitable return on future resource developments.

The claims process proceeded more slowly in the Mackenzie River valley. The seemingly urgent need to develop the Mackenzie corridor as a pipeline route came into direct conflict with Dene, Métis, and Inuit demands that Treaties 8 and 11 be reopened. The priority assigned to oil exploration and development gave the native people a special bargaining weapon.

Southern sympathy for native claims, led by an active church-based lobby, added weight to northern demands. The federal government responded, in classic Canadian fashion in 1974, by appointing Justice Thomas Berger to head the Mackenzie Valley Pipeline Inquiry. Berger ignored the conventions of royal commissions, which typically stayed in southern media centres, and instead hauled his troupe of researchers, intervenors, and reporters into virtually every community potentially affected by the proposed pipeline.

The Berger extravaganza had a stunning impact on southern attitudes toward northern development and native rights. For weeks, the evening news recorded the eloquent testimony of northern natives, often delivered in halting, imperfect English. The deep commitment of Indians and Inuit to their aboriginal rights shone through clearly, both in the testimony and in Berger's final report, which called for the settlement of native land claims and a ten year moratorium on pipeline development. The Alaska Highway Pipeline Inquiry, established to examine the social and economic implications of the Foothills proposal for a natural gas pipeline from Alaska to the south via the highway, had a similar, though less pronounced impact on the Yukon claims process. The final report of the commission, headed by Kenneth Lysyk, was issued in 1977.

Responding to the heightened interest in the Mackenzie River valley and driven by the immediate threat to their way of life, the Dene Assembly in 1975, issued their "Dene Declaration." This document represented a startling elevation of the entire aboriginal rights negotiation process. The document starts,

> We the Dene of the N.W.T. insist on the right to be regarded by ourselves and the world as a nation....The government of Canada is not the government of the Dene. The Government of the N.W.T. is not the government of the Dene...there are realities we are

forced to submit to, such as the existence of a country called Canada, [but] we insist on the right to self-determination as a distinct people...We the Dene are part of the Fourth World...What we seek then is independence and self-determination within the country of Canada.

Federal negotiators backed away from these demands for "province-like" status, shaken by the uncharacteristic and apparent radicalism of the Dene leaders. While the Yukon and other native group claims proceeded through negotiations, the Dene demands lanquished. Even other native groups recoiled at the seemingly excessive requests. The Métis Association of the Northwest Territories broke away from the Dene and, in 1977, tendered a separate claim to the federal government.

The Inuit of the Mackenzie Delta, similarly threatened by the rapid push to develop Beaufort Sea oil, responded through the Committee for Original People's Entitlement. The Inuit in this area had initially negotiated with the larger Inuit Tapirisat of Canada on a united Inuit claim, but the pressures of oil development and the need for a rapid settlement encouraged the Mackenzie Delta people to form their own organization. The COPE claim lacked the radicalism of the Dene document. This request, entitled Inuvialuit Nunangat, called for local government, a sharing of resource revenues, financial compensation for lost rights, and Inuit ownership of 180,000 square kilometres of land and 133,000 square kilometres of water in the western Arctic. The moderate tone of the document and the government's determination to settle the issue in order to expedite oil drilling allowed negotiations to proceed smoothly. An agreement was signed early in 1984, granting about one half the land claimed and $45 million in financial compensation (1977 dollars), with additional funds for economic and social development. The accord also guaranteed the Inuit specific hunting and trapping rights, and promised Inuit participation in future development plans.

The Inuit Tapirisat (or Tungavik Federation), representing the people of Nunavut [central and eastern Arctic], presented its first formal comprehensive claim proposal to the federal government in 1976. The draft was revised several times — partly to purge the document of many of the recommendations of non-native consultants. Like the Dene, Métis, and Yukon claims, however, the negotiations remain unresolved.

Overriding and interfering with land claims negotiations were frequent disputes within and among the many native organizations: for example, whether non-status and/or Métis peoples should be included in the negotiations. Debates over who should be eligible to claim the benefits of a land claims settlement continue to this day in many areas. And there are other problems, like overlapping of claims. The COPE claim, for instance, covered lands also requested by the Yukon Indians, Dene, and Tungavik Federation. Conflicting claims like these have proved difficult to resolve and provided a further impediment to negotiations, allowing the government to stall the process even longer and leave the northern claims issue substantially unresolved.

The natives' response to post-war developments troubled federal officials, white territorial politicians and business people alike. They were accustomed to complacent natives. Many ascribed the new militancy to the work of southern agitators, but efforts to depreciate the native movement ignored the maturity of the

Indian and Inuit positions. The new native leaders, often graduates of the residential schools and frequently university educated, debated effectively on southern terms, but did so with the special conviction of a threatened people. The south's frontier was *their* homeland. A battle thus joined would not soon end.

Demands for Responsible Government

The confrontation over native ownership rights was not the only political struggle in the new north. The territories had long been ignored in the decision-making process. With the exception of limited representatiion on the Yukon Council, and a single Member of Parliament representing the Yukon, the north enjoyed virtually no input in the federal political process. With the boom on, major decisions affecting the north arose, to be dealt with in Ottawa, by civil servants in the north, or by the managers of southern corporations. Northern residents had been hard pressed to challenge this colonial position before 1945. Bolstered by media attention and southern interest in northern resources, territorial demands for a legitimate share of power could no longer be totally ignored.

Representation in the House of Commons was granted grudgingly. A 1947 attempt to have a single Member of Parliament represent a combined Yukon-Mackenzie River valley constituency proved unpopular. Before the 1952 election, separate Yukon and Northwest Territories constituencies were established. The situation remained unchanged until 1979, when the Eastern Arctic received its own representative. These additions improved access to Canada's most important political forum. In fact, the north received far greater representation than the population warranted.

The three representatives did not, however, carry much clout in Parliament, and the north could never rely on such modest regional representation to keep northern concerns on the nation's agenda.

The Yukon's political adolescence proved difficult. The title of Commissioner was resurrected in 1952. The appointments of Yukon residents Gordon Cameron in 1962 and James Smith in 1966 cheered local politicians, but left federal power over territorial affairs intact. Consultation often proved to be a one-way street, and regional anger over Ottawa's high-handed tactics mounted. Federal officials seemed not to see any legitimacy in territorial demands and continued to drag their heels. Elected councillors passed an ''Autonomy motion'' in 1967 and requested a gradual evolution to provincial status. The federal government balked at this suggestion, but did move gradually to improve local consultation. An executive committee was established in 1969 to assist the Commissioner, although a majority of its members remained appointed. Only in 1977 did elected members take over the executive committee, establishing, in effect, a territorial cabinet for the first time. Party politics also arrived. The Conservatives won eleven of sixteen seats in the 1978 electioon and, with Chris Pearson as their leader, they assumed control of the Yukon's administrative apparatus.

The election of the federal Progressive Conservative government in 1979 provided another boost in the lengthy battle for responsible government. Eric Nielsen, who had represented the Yukon since 1958, was a member of the short-lived cabinet of Prime Minister Joseph Clark. Largely through Nielsen's efforts, the federal cabinet agreed to grant responsible government to the Yukon. The power of the Commissioner declined accordingly, as political authority passed, finally, to elected representatives. Then the drive toward provincial status — only half-heartedly supported by most Yukon residents — stalled with the defeat of the Clark government.

The Northwest Territories followed much the same path, at a slower pace. The Territorial Council clung to its Ottawa base, although regional voters elected three of the eight councillors, and the board obligingly met in the territory once a year after 1951. The addition of elected representatives improved the balance until, by 1956, elected councillors held a majority. The Carrothers Commission, formally known as the Advisory Commission on the Development of Government in the Northwest Territories, brought down its report in 1966, and recommended several changes in the administrative structure. The commission rejected Inuit requests that the territory be split into districts reflecting natural and human boundaries. It did, however, recommend that the Territorial Council be permanently established in Yellowknife. The report urged greater local control over administrative matters, but called on the federal government to retain its authority over resources and economic development. The recommendations, many of which were acted upon, resulted in the acceptance of the Northwest Territories as a political entity but left it under the control of the federal government. The Council, relocated in Yellowknife in 1967, was slowly enlarged, and by 1974 was fully elected. Cabinet-style government, although as yet without party politics, had arrived.

By the end of the 1970s, new battle lines had been drawn. Native groups and territorial politicians alike chafed against southern development priorities and political domination. Different conceptions of the northern territories held by native groups, regional politicians, and the federal government, were raised and debated. Little had been resolved, however, leaving the political future of Canada's colonies very much in doubt.

8
Whither the North

The decade after the Berger Commission was not an auspicious one for the Canadian north. The euphoria of the early 1970s has dissipated in the face of political and economic change. Issues which seemed so urgent only a few years ago no longer sit near the top of the country's political agenda. Yet there is a difference from earlier periods of interest in the region — this time, the problems of the north are not likely to fade quietly away.

The north, for example, reappeared briefly in the national consciousness in the summer and fall of 1985. The government's promise to rebuild the Distant Early Warning Line, at a cost of hundreds of millions of dollars, was widely touted as an example of Canada's determination to assert its control over the country's north. That partially positive sign — the radar system was, after all, part of the larger American defence network — was soon offset by more troubling developments. A U.S. ice-breaker, the *Polar Sea*, was sent on a voyage through the northwest passage. The Americans refused to recognize Canada's claim to the northern waters, and declared the passage an international strait. As it had done so often in the past on matters of sovereignty in the north, the federal government vacillated — while the voyage proceeded. Politicians clamoured, after the fact, to demonstrate their dedication to protecting Canada's claim to the high Arctic, dusting off plans for an impressive new icebreaker to carry the country's flag north, promising a new Arctic islands national park, and declaring the government's intention to maintain a higher profile in the area. It took the actions of another country to stimulate a national debate on Canada's northern responsibilities, but the widespread demands for federal initiatives demonstrated surprising national interest in this regional controversy.

Recent economic developments, in particular, have also dampened earlier enthusiastic projections for the region's future. Although the Liberal government's National Energy Programme carried all the old elements of colonial domination of the territorial economies, it nonetheless signalled the primary importance assigned to the north in national economic development. A recession, escalating costs, stable oil prices, poor drilling results in the Beaufort, and difficulties convincing native and environmental groups of the safety of the projects, all undercut the viability of the more grandiose schemes. Yet drilling continues. The federal government permitted Interprovincial (NW) Pipeline to build a shortened pipeline linking the Norman Wells oilfield with the general Canadian trans-shipment grid. The project is much reduced from the larger Mackenzie River valley pipeline or an Alaska Highway natural gas pipeline plan.

Northerners have become accustomed to the abandonment of expansion projects when regional resources declined in value or when southern promoters lost interest. Far more serious has been the apparent disintegration of the foundations of the territorial economy, particularly in the Yukon. United Keno Hill has operated intermittently of late, a victim of falling prices and a bitter and prolonged labour dispute, and White-horse Copper ceased its mining operations.

The closure in 1984 of the Cypress Anvil property near Faro was the cruelest blow. This single mine, responsible for as much as 40 per cent of the territory's economic production, succumbed to declining demand and the unwillingness of the parent company to support the mine and the community. There is another, more subtle irony. The parent firm was none other than Dome Petroleum. Dome purchased a controlling interest in Cypress Anvil as part of its takeover of another oil company. It tried unsuccessfully to sell the mine and refused to commit more money to the property. The mine was officially closed in December 1984, and the few people remaining at Faro began to leave.

Despite such set-backs, or perhaps because of them, the impetus for constitutional improvements continues, although northerners are far from united on the goals or methods of reform.

The debate over the proposed division of the Northwest Territories provides an excellent case in point. Residents of the NWT, particularly in the eastern Arctic, have been asking for several decades for political division. The main proposal would see the larger territory divided roughly between the Mackenzie River Valley and Nunavut, the lands north of the treeline. The purpose was to provide a political structure more sensitive to regional variations in economy and culture. Although there seemed to be general support for the idea, many questions remained. The bulk of potential oil and gas wealth appeared to be in Nunavut, leaving the western district without future resource revenues. Dividing up the administrative apparatus, centred in Yellowknife, created other difficulties.

The Northwest Territories did hold a referendum on the question in 1984. It went in favour of division, and a constitutional forum representing Nunavut and the western district was created to discuss the mechanics of division. The promising start soon faltered when disputes arose over the proposed boundary line. Several coastal communities in the western Arctic, technically included in Nunavut, had strong ties with Mackenzie River communities like Inuvik, and worried about being under the political control of a government located in the far distant eastern Arctic. These debates left a cloud of uncertainty over the question of division.

The demands of the native people, like the proposed division, received considerable support from the Assembly of the N.W.T. Although the Dene Nation (which represents the Dene of the Northwest Territories), and other native groups initially opposed the territorial legislature, they soon recognized its potential for furthering the native cause. Native leaders like James Wah-See, Richard Nerysoo, and Tagak Curley were elected to the assembly and used this new forum to push their demands. Specific efforts were made to work with native groups — a ''Committee on Unity'' was formed to coordinate activities — and assistance was given to the native positions in negotiations with the federal government.

In the Yukon Territory, poor relations between native organizations and territorial politicians have interfered with political change. The Conservative administration intervened at several points in the native land claims process, blocking negotiations in an attempt to have their own concerns added to the federal government's agenda. The Conservatives' preoccupation with immediate economic development, particularly the proposed pipeline, did not sit well with native groups demanding greater control of resources and a larger say in the development process. The result was political disunity, and two different interpretations of the territory's future direction. The surprise election of a New Democratic Party minority government in 1985 ended the Conservative Party's grip on the Territorial Council and suggested that a new direction in territorial policy might be forthcoming.

Regional problems have seldom been the major stumbling blocks to the resolution of northern political concerns. Recent developments pertaining to native land claims illustrate the exceptional and continuing vulnerability of the north to the agendas of southern politicians. Early in 1984, the Committee for Original People's Entitlement signed an agreement with the Liberal administration, a positive sign that federal-native negotiations were finally bearing fruit. The Council of Yukon Indians and the federal government signed an agreement in principle in June 1984, apparently bringing to an end twelve difficult years of bargaining. The final deal, subject to continuing discussions on several outstanding points, had to be signed by 31 December 1984. It was not. A federal election and a change in government intervened. The CYI Annual General Assembly in August 1984 asked for a renegotiation of several key points, including the government's determination to extinguish aboriginal title through the accord and a different formula for land selection. David Crombie, the new Minister of Indian Affairs and Northern Development, initially indicated that negotiations would continue, but then decided to stick by the end-of-the-year deadline for agreement. The new year began without an accord; years of tough bargaining had come to a bitterly disappointing end.

While the political energy of the 1970s may be lacking in the 1980s, considerable organizational support for social justice in the north remains. The long-standing commitment of the major Christian churches to native matters has shifted from earlier attempts to restructure Indian society to a position of solidarity with native organizations. The inter-church organization Project North, founded in 1975, holds a continuing watch on northern and native matters, providing research and political support as required. Environmental groups have similarly picked up on Berger's warnings about the possible effects of northern development, and numerous national organizations monitor business and government activities in the Yukon and Northwest Territories. One particularly respected and influential organization, the Canadian Arctic Resources Committee, supports a broad programme of public education, research, and informed political intervention on northern matters. The political authority of territorial and native leaders has been repeatedly augmented by the skill and commitment of such southern Canadian supporters. The intervention of Project North, Canadian Arctic Resources Committee and other organizations, for example, succeeded in stopping Gulf Oil's planned construction of a shipping facility at Stokes Point, west of the Mackenzie River.

The Need for a New Northern Vision

The historical experience of the Canadian North makes it very clear that something must be done to alter the entrenched colonial pattern. Few are optimistic about the prospects for significant change. Gurston Dacks, a political scientist, ended his study of northern politics — aptly titled *A Choice of Futures* — on a most pessimistic note:

The end result will be federal policies that leave the North where Ottawa has always left it - in the wilderness. While a choice of futures does arguably remain for the North at the start of the 1980s, the odds are that the die is cast. In Ottawa, the purposeful drift will accelerate. In the North, the costs of economic dependence will remain very much in evidence. The frustrations of colonial politics, while diminished, will persist — an apparently permanent feature of the northern political landscape.

Farley Mowat, writing in *Canada North Now*, first released in 1967, stated the case with greater passion:

Through many generations, we Southerners have smugly sung of a great nation stretching from the eastern sea to the western sea. It is past time for us to realize that Canada stretches to the northern sea as well; and if we are to remain either strong *or* free we must embrace the reality of our northern realm, making it truly an integral part of the nation instead of continuing to treat it as a mere colonial appendage which we may allow others to bleed to death with impunity. If we have any survival sense at all, we will put an end to the Great Northern Giveaway and bring a halt to the despoliation of the northern lands and waters, and to the degradation of the northern peoples. If there be any conscience in us, we will begin making amends for the disasters we have already wrought in that far country.

It would be facile to suggest that quick or simple solutions are either possible or desirable. Most would agree, however, that the unending cycle of boom and bust should be broken. Putting "Canadian" needs high on the priority list does not mean that regional concerns can be disregarded. With the possible exception of

Arctic oil, it appears unlikely that any single discovery or even combination of developments in the north will miraculously cure Canada's economic woes. Canadians will have to find a more realistic appraisal of the north's potential. Properly managed and carefully developed with an eye to environmental safety, native needs and regional economic requirements, northern resources could sustain a moderately-sized population and bring some semblance of stability ot a very unstable region.

Territorial politicians often speak of provincial status. Such proposals quickly generate a negative response from federal politicians and southern Canadians. A Province of Yukon with fewer than 25,000 people? Two provinces in what is now the Northwest Territories? Can Canada make provinces of jurisdictions almost totally dependent on federal grants?

It is not in fact clear that northerners want provincial status. In the Northwest Territories, the demand has not been extensively debated, except in conjunction with the Nunavut proposal. In the Yukon divisions between natives and whites, and concerns over the district's ability to handle the political and financial responsibilities of provincial status, continue to dampen enthusiasm for the proposition. Proponents claim that control over resources would provide the territory with sufficient revenue to stand on its own (It is worth noting that the anticipated dependence on federal transfer payments would not make the Yukon any more vulnerable than several of Canada's poorer provinces.) It is, however, unlikely that the federal government will surrender ownership of resources.

More to the point, it is not at all clear that provincial status is in the north's best interest. Because of its economic and political vulnerability, the Yukon and

Northwest Territories — as provinces — would have little authority at the nation's bargaining tables. If the north were made "equal" in a constitutional sense, it would actually lose power since the federal government would no longer feel compelled to defend the region. The north, in fact, requires the assistance, perhaps even protection, of a more benevolent federal state, one that would represent the interests of the region rather than looking at its resources as a "quick fix" for the economy.

Talk of provincial status remains on hold. Several additional changes need not await a resolution of these broader constitutional questions. The first item on the agenda is, clearly, a resolution of outstanding native land claims. The federal government will have to put aside the adversarial approach to negotiations. The new Yukon government, more supportive of the native position, will likely assist the process much like the N.W.T. Assembly has done. Native organizations will have to acknowledge the limits to what they can logically or justifiably expect. It is naïve to anticipate that native organizations alone will be granted extensive administrative powers. Any just settlement, however, should provide for greater autonomy over native matters, remove from bureaucratic purview many aspects of native life and culture, and guarantee native peoples a say in, and a reasonable return from, future resource developments. Until the land claims issue is resolved, other political and economic changes are unlikely.

It is similarly possible to grant both territorial administrations greater freedom without granting provincial status. Ottawa has in the past negotiated independently with corporations planning northern projects, informing regional politicians only when the final agreements have been signed. Northern politicians can be formally incorporated into the decision-making process, given a powerful voice on federal departmental planning committees and assured of a place in all future negotiations affecting the region. Northern input could be assured on all boards, committees, and in all negotiations involving specifically territorial affairs. It may be some time before southern politicians and bureaucrats are prepared to accept that northern representatives have a great deal to offer to national deliberations; in the interim, they should acknowledge that regional officials know (typically far better than Ottawa-based civil servants) what is best for their region.

It would help, too, if federal decision-making personnel and power were shifted from Ottawa to the territorial capitals, so that those people representing the "national interest" would become more familiar with local conditions, and local politicians and territorial civil servants could more adequately defend their interests. Speaking of his province in 1903, British Columbia Premier E. Prior noted, "Victoria is 3,000 miles from Ottawa whereas Ottawa is 30,000 miles from Victoria." This attitude applies equally today in the Canadian North.

Together these modest suggestions for political change — more matters of atttitude than outright constitutional reform — call for a redefinition of Canada's national interest in the north. As long as gold-edged visions of northern resources continue to dominate southern perceptions, little is likely to change. The past has demonstrated that when these visions fade or are tarnished by economic depression, the impetus for significant political restructuring will similarly disappear. It remains, as always, a matter of political will. If the federal government is truly interested in eliminating the last remnants of its colonial heritage, and granting the Yukon and Northwest Territories their just level of political autonomy, then constitutional, administrative, and financial answers can be found to all existing questions. The colonial way, unfortunately, tends toward bureaucratic lethargy; entrenched political and administrative power structures often prove an amazingly resilient barrier to significant change. One can only hope that the lessons offered by the history of Canada's colonies will not be forgotten, and will be used to build a better future for the Yukon and the Northwest Territories.

Further Reading

The following is intended as a preliminary guide for those readers interested in pursuing further the history of Canada's north.

Introduction

The best attempt to address the role of the Canadian north in the Canadian mind is Louis-Edmond Hamelin, *Canadian Nordicity: It's Your North, Too* (Montreal, 1978). Also useful are Carl Berger, "The True North Strong and Free," in Peter Russell, *Nationalism in Canada* (Toronto, 1966) and W.L. Morton, "The North in Canadian Historiography," in A.B. McKillop, ed., *Contexts of Canada's Past* (Toronto, 1980). For an overview of historical work on the north, see K. Coates and W.R. Morrison, "Northern Visions: Recent Historical Writing on the Canadian North," *Manitoba History* (Fall 1985).

There are only a few general studies of the history of the region. Morris Zaslow, *The Opening of the Canadian North, 1870-1914* (Toronto, 1971) is rich in detail and insight. His short pamphlet, *The Northwest Territories, 1905-1980* (Ottawa, 1984) is also useful. For an overview of the economic development of the north, Kenneth Rea, *The Political Economy of the Canadian North* (Toronto, 1968) is the best place to start. Also helpful is Peter Usher, "The North: Metropolitan Frontier, Native Homeland," in L.D.

McCann, *Heartland and Hinterland* (Scarborough, 1982).

1: The Land, Original Peoples and First Contacts

Those wishing a more complete description of the northern landscape can begin with John Warkentin, ed. *Canada: A Regional Geography* (Toronto, 1968). There is an immense literature on pre-contact native societies. A good place to start is James VanStone, *Athapaskan Adaptations* (Chicago, 1974) and Alice Kehoe, ''The Arctic and the Subarctic'' in *North American Indians* (Englewood Cliffs, 1981). For more detailed information, see June Helm, ed. *Handbook of North American Indians, vol. v: The Subarctic,* (Washington, 1981). Marshall Sahlins, ''The Original Affluent Society,'' in *Stone Age Economics* (Aldine, 1972) provides a unique perspective on harvesting societies.

There is similarly a great deal of material available on European exploration. Journals or memoirs are available for most major explorations. For a general approach to the field, A. Cooke and C. Holland, *The Exploration of Northern Canada, 500 to 1920: A Chronology* (Toronto, 1978) is indispensable. On the early explorers, see T. Oleson's controversial *Early Voyages, Northern Approaches* (Toronto, 1968). L.H. Neatby, *In Quest of the North West Passage* (Toronto, 1958) surveys the major explorations. The best book on northern exploration is probably H. Wallace, *The Navy, the Company and Richard King* (Montreal, 1980).

There is, similarly, a number of studies of fur trade expansion into the northwest. The most useful source is T. Karamanski, *Fur Trade and Exploration: Opening the Far Northwest, 1821-1852* (Vancouver, 1983).

A.A. Wright's, *Prelude to Bonanza* (Sidney, 1976) looks more specifically at the early Yukon explorers.

2: The Early Fur Trade

For the general background to the northern fur trade, see H. Innis, *The Fur Trade in Canada* (Toronto, 1975) and E.E. Rich, *The Fur Trade and the Northwest to 1857* (Toronto, 1976). Two other books, A.J. Ray, *Indians in the Fur Trade* (Toronto, 1974) and Robin Fisher, *Contact and Conflict* (Vancouver, 1976) are also very helpful.

The northward advance of the fur trade can be followed in W. Sloan, "The Native Response to the Extension of the European Traders into the Athabasca and Mackenzie Basin, 1770-1814," *Canadian Historical Review* (Fall 1979), J.C. Yerbury, "The Nahanny Indians and the Fur Trade, 1800-1840," *Musk-ox* (1981), S. Krech III, "The Eastern Kutchin and the Fur Trade, 1800-1869," *Ethnohistory* (1976); and Ken Coates, "Furs Along the Yukon: Hudson's Bay Company - Native Trade in the Yukon River Valley, 1840-1893," *BC Studies* (Autumn 1982).

Specific aspects of the social and economic changes brought by the fur trade are covered in A.J. Ray, "Competition and Conservation in the Early Subarctic Fur Trade," *Ethnohistory* (1978); S. Krech III, "Throwing Bad Medicine: Sorcery, Disease and the Fur Trade Among the Kutchin and other Northern Athapaskans," in Krech, ed. *Indians, Animals and the Fur Trade* (Athens, 1982), S. Krech III, "On the Aboriginal Population of the Kutchin," *Arctic Anthropology* (1978); and S. Krech III, ed. *The Subarctic Fur Trade: Native Economic and Social Adaptations* (Vancouver, 1984), which includes A. J. Ray's provocative article, "Periodic Shortages, Native Welfare and the Hudson's Bay Company, 1670-1930."

The activities of northern missionaries can be traced in J. W. Grant, *The Moon of Wintertime* (Toronto, 1984). A recent dissertation by Kerry Abel, "The Drum and the Cross: An Ethnohistorical Study of Mission Work Among the Dene, 1858-1902," (Queen's, 1984) provides a new perspective on native spirituality and the advance of Christianity. Also of help is Frank Peake's "Fur Traders and Missionaries," *Western Canadian Journal of Anthropology* (1977).

3: The Gold Frontier and the Klondike

The British Columbia background to the northern mining frontier can be found in S.D. Clark, "Mining Society in British Columbia and the Yukon," in W.P. Ward and R.A.J. McDonald, *British Columbia: Historical Readings* (Vancouver, 1981) and "British Columbia," in R. C. Harris and J. Warkentin, *Canada Before Confederation* (Toronto, 1974).

On the early Yukon gold frontier, see T. Stone, "Flux and Authority in a Subarctic Society: The Yukon Miners in the Nineteenth Century," *Ethnohistory* (1983), T. Stone, "Atomistic Order and Frontier Violence: Miners and Whalemen in the Nineteenth Century Yukon," *Ethnology* (October 1983), and T. Stone, "The Mounties as Vigilantes: Reflections on Community and the Transformation of Law in the Yukon, 1885-1897," *Law and Socety Review* (1974). For a contrary view on Canadian authority, see W. R. Morrison, *Showing the Flag: The Mounted Police and Canadian Sovereignty in the North, 1895-1925* (Vancouver, 1985).

On the gold rush itself, P. Berton's anecdotal *Klondike Fever* (New York, 1958) and J.D. MacGregor,

The Klondike Rush Through Edmonton (Toronto, 1970) are interesting. The role of the federal government can best be traced in D. Hall, *Clifford Sifton*, 2 vols. (Vancouver, 1982 and 1984). Also useful is Lewis Green, *The Gold Hustlers* (Anchorage, 1976), which documents the take-over of the goldfields by the concessionaires. David Morrison, *The Politics of the Yukon Territory, 1898-1909* (Toronto, 1968) decribes the chaotic political life in the goldfields.

4: Doldrums in the Middle North

This period has largely been ignored by historians. On the Yukon, the insightful memoirs of Laura Berton, *I Married the Klondike* (Toronto, 1954) and Martha Black, *My Seventy Years* (London, 1938) are a good place to start. Gordon Bennett's *Yukon Transportation: A History* (Ottawa, 1978) describes changes in river and land transportation in this era.

There is more material available on government-native relations. See, for example, René Fumoleau, *As Long As This Land Shall Last* (Toronto, 1976); Ken Coates, "Best Left as Indians: Government-Native Relations in the Yukon Territory, 1894-1950," *Canadian Journal of Native Studies* (Fall 1984); and W. R. Morrison, "The Native People of the Northern Frontier," in H. Dempsey, ed. *Men in Scarlet* (Calgary, 1974). On native education, see A. D. Fisher, "A Colonial Education System: Historical Changes and Schooling in Fort Chipewyan," *Canadian Journal of Anthropology* (1977); and Ken Coates, "Betwixt and Between: The Anglican Church and the Children on the Carcross Residential School, 1910-1950," *BC Studies* (Winter 1984-1985).

The main work on economic history is Kenneth Rea, *The Political Economy of the Canadian North*. Robert

Bothwell's *Eldorado* (Toronto, 1984) describes the interesting history of the development of Port Radium. The most important resource on the fur trade is Peter Usher, *Fur Trade Posts of the Northwest Territories, 1870-1970* (Ottawa, 1971).

5: Boom and Bust in the Arctic

The best work on Arctic whaling is by W. G. Ross. See his major study, *Whaling and Eskimos: Hudson Bay, 1860-1915* (Ottawa, 1975), plus *An Arctic Whaling Diary: The Journal of Captain George Comer* (Toronto, 1984); and "Whaling, Inuit and the Arctic Islands," in Zaslow, *A Century of Canada's Arctic Islands* (Ottawa, 1981). On the Herschel Island experience, see Thomas Stone's, "Whalers and Missionaries at Herschel Island," *Ethnohistory* (1981); and "Atomistic Order and Frontier Violence: Miners and Whalemen in the Nineteenth Century Yukon," *Ethnology* (1983).

On the role of the Canadian government in the Arctic, W. R. Morrison's, *Showing the Flag* is indispensable. Also useful are several of the essays in Zaslow, *A Century of Canada's Arctic Islands*, especially the editor's "Administering the Arctic Islands, 1880-1940." Government-Inuit relations can be traced in Diamond Jenness' classic work, *Eskimo Administration, II: Canada* (Montreal, 1964) and an up-dated study, R. Diubaldo, *The Government and the Inuit* (Ottawa, 1985). V. Stefansson's Arctic career is covered in detail in his autobiography *Discovery* (New York, 1964). More useful is the very careful biography by R. Diubaldo, *Stefansson and the Canadian Arctic* (Montreal, 1978)

Peter Usher's work, including "Canadian Western Arctic," *Anthropologica* (1971); "Growth and Decay of the Trading and Trapping Frontiers in the Western Canadian Arctic,'' *Canadian Geographer* (1975); *Fur Trade Posts of the Northwest Territories*; and *The Bankslanders: Economy and Ecology of a Frontier Trapping Community* (Ottawa, 1970), is central to an understanding of the twentieth century fur trade.

6: The Army's North

For the broader story of Canadian military planning during World War II, see C.P. Stacey, *Arms, Men and Governments* (Ottawa, 1974). On Canadian-American ventures, see S. W. Dziuban, *Military Relations Between the United States and Canada, 1939-1945* (Washington, 1959). David Remley's *The Crooked Road* (Toronto, 1976) provides a largely anecdotal account of the building of the Alaska Highway. The essays in Ken Coates' *The Alaska Highway* (Vancouver, 1985) provide much useful information on many aspects of highway construction.

For other defence projects, see R. Diubaldo, ''The Canol Project in Canadian-American Relations,'' Canadian Historical Association, *Historical Papers* (1977), Diubaldo, ''The Role of the Arctic Islands in Defence,'' in M. Zaslow, *A Century of Canada's Arctic Islands*, and Diubaldo and S. Scheinberg, *A Study of Canadian-American Defence Policy* (Ottawa, 1976).

7 & 8: The Bureaucrats' North and Whither the North

Historians are just beginning to address the ''new'' north. There are, however, a variety of useful studies which cover the major themes in the contemporary north. The native land claims debate can be approached through W. R. Morrison, *A Survey of the History and*

Claims of the Native Peoples of Northern Canada (Ottawa, 1985). Also useful are H. and K. McCullum, *This Land is Not For Sale* (Toronto, 1975); H. Brody, *The People's Land* (Harmondsworth, 1975), M. Watkins, ed. *Dene Nation — the colony within* (Toronto, 1977); M. Asch, *Home and Native Land* (Agincourt, 1984); and P. Cumming, *Canada: Native Land Rights and Northern Development* (Copenhagen, 1977). The classic statement, of course, is T. Berger, *Northern Frontier, Northern Homeland* (Ottawa, 1977).

There is also a rapidly expanding literature on northern development and political change. J. Lotz, *Northern Realities* (Toronto, 1970) is now rather dated, but remains useful. Edgar Dosman, ed. *The Arctic in Question* (Toronto, 1976); E. Dosman, *The National Interest: The Politics of Northern Development, 1968-1978* (Toronto, 1978); M. O'Malley, *The Past and Future Land* (Toronto, 1976); and F. Bergha, *Bob Blair's Pipeline* (Toronto, 1979) offered detailed accounts of current controversies. The best survey of political events in the contemporary north is G. Dacks, *A Choice of Futures* (Toronto, 1981).

Index

Books in the Canadian Issues Series

Police
Urban Policing in Canada
JOHN SEWELL

This informative primer by Canada's best-known urban reformer, John Sewell, fills the information vacuum that reduces most discussion of policing to "for" or "against". The book begins with an outline history of policing and a discussion of the "true" extent of crime. Sewell then turns to the day-to-day issues of policing, from the effectiveness of patrol work to the drawbacks of rigid police hierarchies.

"A handy elementary guide to the basics of policing today." — Montreal *Gazette*.

The West
The History of a Region in Confederation
J.F. CONWAY

Since settlers first tried to eke out a living on the banks of the Red River, Western Canadians have felt that the West's place in the Canadian scheme of things is a subordinate one. John Conway's book is a history of Confederation from the point of view of the four western provinces. Conway shows that although the focus of western dissatisfaction may have changed in recent years, the root problem of having to "buy dear and sell cheap" remains.

"A must for anyone who wishes to know about the recent economic and political past of Western Canada." — Lethbridge *Herald*.

Ethics and Economics
Canada's Catholic Bishops on the Economic Crisis
GREGORY BAUM AND DUNCAN CAMERON

The most talked-about political manifesto of recent years is "Ethical Reflections on the Economic Crisis," issued in early 1983 by Canada's Catholic bishops. This book takes the issues raised by the bishops several steps further. "Ethical Reflections" is included, followed by two wide-ranging commentaries: one from an ethical point of view, by Gregory Baum; the other from an economic perspective, by Duncan Cameron. Several earlier statements by the bishops are also included, as is a guide to further reading on this subject.

"A major contribution to the understanding of the Canadian Church." — *Catholic New Times*.

Oil and Gas
Ottawa, the Provinces and the Petroleum Industry
JAMES LAXER

For more than a decade, the oil industry and energy policy have been a central issue in Canadian economic and political life. *Oil and Gas* offers an overview of these turbulent years and fresh insight into the motives of the main players: Ottawa, Alberta and other producing provinces, the oil majors such as Imperial, the Canadian companies like Petro-Canada, the OPEC cartel and the U.S. government.

"Provocative reading" — *Canadian Public Policy*.

Women and Work
Inequality in the Labour Market
PAUL PHILLIPS AND ERIN PHILLIPS

Why are women still second-class citizens at work? To answer this question, Paul and Erin Phillips trace women's involvement in the paid labour market, and in labour unions, throughout Canadian history. They document the disadvantages that women face today and examine the explanations that have been forwarded for the persistence of these problems. Chapters are devoted to the effect of technological changes such as the microelectronic "chip" on women's work, and to proposals for bringing about equality in the labour market.

"A fine salute to the strong body of materials on women's work that has sprung into being in the last decade." — Toronto *Star*.

Regional Disparities
New Updated Edition
Paul Phillips

This is the first and only book to address the perennial problem of the gap between "have" and "have-not" provinces. In this new updated edition of his popular study, Paul Phillips examines developments such as the National Energy Program, the Alberta-Ottawa oil deal, the industrial slump in Central Canada, and the increased prospects for economic growth in resource-rich provinces.

"A concise, convincing overview." — *Quill & Quire*.

The New Canadian Constitution

DAVID MILNE

The New Canadian Constitution explains just what everyone wanted out of the constitution-making process, who got what, and what the final results mean for Canadians. Of special interest is the concluding chapter, which examines the nature of the new constitution in terms of both the interests, issues and accidents that shaped it, and its own strengths and weaknesses.

"...a straightforward and comprehensive narrative." — *Globe and Mail*.

Industry in Decline

RICHARD STARKS

Summing up proposals from labour, the NDP, the business community and the Science Council of Canada, Richard Starks, a financial journalist formerly with the *Financial Post*, examines the growing consensus that Canada needs a new industrial strategy.

"The beauty of the book and its importance is its straightforward, uncomplicated, journalistic style, and its price." — *Canadian Materials*.

Rising Prices

H. LUKIN ROBINSON

This book explains why prices are so high today and tells us what inflation is all about. The author defines mystifying terms like "cost-push" inflation and applies them to everyday situations.

"A masterpiece of popular economics. This book swiftly moves from the very elementary to the very complex...without losing its readers along the way." — *Canadian Forum*.

Out of Work

CY GONICK

Cy Gonick shows why the Canadian economy is failing to create jobs for all the people who want to work and why government is unwilling to take the necessary steps to deal with the issue.

"Gonick is one of the few political scientists around who can put complicated arguments into readable English. He talks more sense in less space than any other contemporary commentator." — *Books in Canada*.

Other Books of Interest from James Lorimer & Company

Bob Blair's Pipeline
The Business and Politics of Northern Energy Development Projects
FRANÇOIS BREGHA

In this study the pipeline saga, François Bregha provides a fascinating look at the economics and politics of resource development in Canada, illuminating the world of corporate business and the roles the National Energy Board, federal bureaucracies and politicians play as the country gropes toward an energy strategy.

"Bregha gives us a thorough history of the project and why its form has changed over time...a fascinating insight into the politics of pipelines." — Regina *Leader-Post*.

Canada and the Reagan Challenge
Crisis and Adjustment, 1981-1985
STEPHEN CLARKSON

In this updated edition of his acclaimed study of the crisis in Canada-U.S. relations, Stephen Clarkson argues that the final years of the Liberal administration achieved equilibrium in dealing with Ronald Reagan's Washington on many contentious bilateral issues. But this stability is jeopardized by the continentalist stand of the new Conservative government in Ottawa.

"Canadians, including the Prime Minister, should read, or reread this book." — Patrick Martin, *Globe and Mail*.

Canadian Churches and Social Justice

Edited by JOHN R. WILLIAMS

Canadian churches are taking an increasingly active role in a wide range of public issues. In this important book, John Williams has selected key statements from a variety of churches and ecumenical bodies and provided an insightful introduction to each. The issues dealt with are poverty and unemployment; capitalism and corporations; nuclear energy; northern development and native peoples; Canada, Quebec and the constitution; population, refugees and immigrants; and Canada and the Third World.

Reservations are for Indians

HEATHER ROBERTSON

Heather Robertson's first book has won wide recognition as an outstanding documentary report on Canada's Native people. *Reservations are for Indians* revolves around life in four Indian communities, but also examines the history of treaty negotiations and the controlling role of the federal government.

"A triumph of the reporter's art: a factual, revealing and profoundly infuriating account of life as most Native peoples of Canada are forced to live it." — Robert Fulford, *Saturday Night*.

Voyage of the Iceberg
The Story of the Iceberg that Sank the Titanic

RICHARD BROWN

This book has established Richard Brown in the ranks of Canada's distinguished nature writers. It is the story of the *Titanic*, and of history's most infamous iceberg.

But there is much more in *Voyage of the Iceberg*. As the iceberg makes its way from Baffin Bay to the fateful meeting in the North Atlantic, it passes through many other lives — of Inuit, whales, whalers and sealers — that Brown portrays in quiet, compelling prose. The acclaim this richly illustrated book has received for the English and French editions in Canada has been echoed by its success in Europe and the United States.

"Lilting, lyrical and loving…a smashing little book."
— Vancouver *Provincer*.